From Where I Sit

A Memoir

Victoria Covington

Published by

In association with RSE Publishing

Copyright © 2014 by Victoria Covington

ISBN 978-1505449525

Library of Congress Control Number: 2014959268

Printed in the United States of America
Edited by Amanda L. Capps
Book Design by Michael Seymour
Cover Design by Dan Fowler

ACKNOWLEDGMENTS

More than five years have elapsed since I began crafting this memoir. The people named below have played significant roles in bringing the project to fruition; innumerable others—no less significant—have cheered me on from the sidelines, offering support, encouragement, and commiseration as needed. To all of them, I extend my profoundly heartfelt gratitude.

FROM WHERE I SIT is the direct result of a (largely unspoken) promise I made to my mother many years ago. Early on, she instilled in me the habit of keeping scrapbooks, thereby ensuring that I would have ready access to the personal memorabilia essential for autobiographical writing. Taking her own advice, she saved a boxful of my letters written to Daddy and her during my University of Illinois years. I have quoted from these extensively in my narrative.

In 2011, ten long-standing friends agreed to read and evaluate my newly completed manuscript: Fay McLaurin, Dady and Martha Mehta, Dean Sanders, Nancy Stagg, John Mramor, Polly McAlpine, Patricia Smith Gumbel, John Fowler, and Gail Willmott. I knew that they would approach their assignment thoughtfully and seriously and that their personal loyalty to me would not preclude a candid assessment of the material. Their unanimously positive endorsements solidified my resolve and validated the worthiness of telling my story.

Two of my reviewers made excellent recommendations for broadening the content of the book. Polly McAlpine suggested that I be more specific about the piano repertoire I studied as a beginner. John Mramor asked what I did for fun as a child and adolescent. That seemingly innocent question led to a greatly expanded, more comprehensive description of those years.

Dady and Martha Mehta were a continual source of perceptive insights. I was delighted when Dady agreed to tell, in his own words, his reaction to my first piano lesson with him—a moment he had literally dreaded!

Dean Sanders's keen eye for detail exposed errors of wording that had escaped previous detection. I had no idea that he had kept many of the letters I had written to him through the years. When he graciously sent them to me, I was able to fill in crucial information missing from my other sources.

Since I was unconscious during the early stages of my E. coli illness, I asked my sister, Mary Jo Covington-Harris, for a detailed account of those events. She then read the opening section of Chapter 14 and verified its accuracy.

My personal aide, Darlene Clark, solved every technology-related problem with her characteristic efficiency and, in the process, elevated my computer skills from minimal to adequate.

In the spring of 2012, serendipity led me to Amanda Capps, a professional writer, editor, and publicist in Greenville, S.C. Under her gentle, persistent guidance, my dry, academic prose gradually took on the color and emotional depth appropriate for a personal memoir. Amanda has also worked tirelessly to promote *FROM WHERE I SIT*, exploring a variety of publishing options and assisting me in making informed decisions about numerous details of which I had no prior knowledge or experience.

Daniel Fowler masterfully designed the cover of the book. Frank Maglione, staff member of the UIUC Rehabilitation Center, took the cover photograph on February 20, 1975, during my faculty recital at the Krannert Center of the Performing Arts.

I regret that neither of my parents lived to see *FROM WHERE I SIT* in its final form. I believe they would have been pleased; I'm sure they would have been jubilant that—at long last—I got the job done.

WHAT'S IN A NAME?

I love my name—Victoria—but why did my parents choose such a strong, proud name for their tiny, fragile, physically disabled infant whose future seemed uncertain and precarious?

Mother said later she had always liked the name, and Daddy had a childless aunt, Victoria Smith Funkhouser, who would undoubtedly welcome a namesake.

Whatever my parents' reasons, their choice was vindicated. I now tell my "victorious" story as a tribute to my mother, Christine Benfield Covington, whose love and support made my success possible and who told me many times, "Someday, you should write a book!"

CHAPTER ONE

BROKEN WINGS

I GREW UP IN THE GARDEN OF EDEN. No, not that one. I'm talking about the one located three and a half miles east of Bennettsville, on South Carolina Highway No. 9.

After passing Cottingham Creek, even the most casual itinerant must surely notice that the sky is a little bluer, the fields a little greener, the air a little fresher. My Covington forebears first settled here in the 1770s, having received a grant from the King of England himself. Many generations of Covington men, including my daddy, farmed the land. This legacy has engendered in me a strong "sense of place." I've always known where my roots are.

WHEN I MADE my entrance on February 11, 1946, I was obviously not a physically perfect baby. My rigid right wrist pointed downward. Both of my feet turned inward. My right limbs were shorter and less developed than my left. Medical examination revealed that all the joints on my right side and several on my left were malformed in some way, the worst being my right hip, which had no socket. Doctors called my condition a "birth defect."

I never knew exactly how my parents, Harry and Christine Covington, received this news, but I suspect they were stunned and frightened. Their hopes and dreams for me certainly had not included a physical disability. This unforeseen obstacle must have seemed like a slap in the face, throwing into disarray all their plans for my future. However, being sensible, rational people, Mother and Daddy would have quickly realized that the future could wait; first and foremost, they had to seek medical advice and determine how, or if, my abnormalities could be corrected.

Many years later, Mother told me that shortly after I was born, a friend had offered her this reassurance: "Don't worry, Chris. When a baby bird has a broken wing, it may never be able to fly, but it can still sing a beautiful song." Mother said she often recalled those seemingly prophetic words as she watched my musical career blossom and flourish. But even she could not have predicted that her little Vickie would grow up to become Dr. Victoria Covington, a concert pianist and career music teacher.

After consulting several orthopedic surgeons in the Carolinas, Mother and Daddy placed me in the care of Dr. Julian E. Jacobs in Charlotte, North Carolina. Between the ages of one and twelve, my life was punctuated at fairly regular intervals by surgeries to fix my various problems—both heels, left knee, right wrist, and right hip (three times).

Since Mother was allowed to stay with me in my hospital room, I never had to face these harrowing ordeals alone, although not even her presence could diminish the sheer terror I felt every time I had to be put to sleep with the sickening ether. I'd struggle and scream in protest when the anesthesiologist lowered the mask to my face; two strong nurses had to restrain me, because I knew that when I woke up, I'd be nauseous for days.

On one occasion, I did manage to control my hysteria. As I lay in my bed awaiting surgery on my left knee, Sister Maria, one of the hospital's kindly nuns, entered my room and told Mother she wanted to speak with me. Mother discreetly left us alone. I considered all the nuns to be my friends, but Sister Maria and I shared a special bond. She approached me, clad totally in white. I remember thinking that she lacked only the wings of an angel.

Gazing straight into my eyes, she spoke gently: "Vickie, you're a very brave girl, but I'm going to ask you to be even more brave. Do you think you can stay calm and relaxed when you're being put to sleep?"

I gulped, drew a deep breath, and flinched slightly.

"If you're calm," she continued, "the ether will work more quickly, and you won't be as sick when you wake up." I saw her glance at the baby doll nestled in the covers next to me. "If you try really hard not to cry," she added, "I'll give you a new doll."

How could I refuse such a generous offer from one of my favorite people? I nodded and gave my solemn promise to do my best.

When the dreaded moment came, I did shed a few tears, but no restraint was necessary. Sister Maria must have thought I held up my end of the bargain, because when I opened my eyes, I saw

my new doll—not a baby, but a "young lady" doll, wearing a pale blue dress and a pearl necklace. Today, I still awake each morning to see her smiling at me from my bedside table. She has a new dress, but her original pearls remain shiny and lustrous.

Relaxing at a friend's house in Myrtle Beach following hip surgery. I've never understood why my legs were set in such an awkward position.

3

My surgeries were ordeals for Mother too. Having seen me through the trauma of hospitalization, she then took sole responsibility for my recuperations after I went home. I usually had to wear a cast for six to eight weeks, followed by additional weeks of relearning to use my limbs. Mother and I became extraordinarily close during those years—and for the next half-century (until the onset of her Alzheimer's in the 1990s), she assumed the role of "enabler," mitigating my physical problems whenever and however she could.

Mother's steadfast courage is all the more remarkable because nothing in Christine Benfield Covington's background prepared her to care for a "special needs" child. She grew up motherless about twenty-five miles east of Bennettsville in the small town of Dillon, South Carolina, with her father, Bunyan Bailey ("B.B.") Benfield, her sister, and two brothers. When B.B.'s wife died in the flu epidemic of 1919, Mother was only a year old. Child care passed to a series of housekeepers who drifted in and out of their lives.

Mother often spoke of the absence of adult supervision in her early years, marveling that she had not become a juvenile delinquent or even a criminal. Having survived this troubled childhood, Mother vowed that someday her children would have in abundance the attention and stability she herself had sorely missed. Her difficult upbringing may account for her insistence on being called Mother, not Mama or Mom. The formal title in no way connoted a lack of warmth or affection, but rather, I think, served as an appropriate symbol of her serious commitment to her maternal responsibilities.

By the time I was born, B.B. was firmly established as the owner of the first two movie theaters at Myrtle Beach. Among my fondest memories are the many weeks Mother and I spent at his house during my post-surgery recuperations. After months of being

4

confined in a cast, I loved sitting at the edge of the ocean, digging in the soft sand, and riding the carousel at the amusement park. B.B.'s natural reticence precluded his being a hands-on grandfather, but I never doubted his love and concern for me. As an adult, I learned that he had paid all of my childhood medical expenses.

FROM 1946-50, MOTHER AND DADDY LIVED WITH MY COVINGTON GRANDPARENTS, Mary Louise (née Smith) and John S. Covington, so "Mamie" and "Gran" were an integral part of my early upbringing. They made a rather odd couple, Mamie's serious reserve contrasting sharply with Gran's ebullience.

Digging in the soft Myrtle Beach sand. This is the only time I ever posed "topless"!

Their imposing two-story white house, located just a stone's throw from Cottingham Creek, seemed to a small child like a castle in a fairy tale with its spacious, if somewhat drafty rooms, antique furnishings, and exotic, fragile bric-a-brac. ("Look, but don't touch," I'd been warned.) My daddy, Harry P. Covington, and his older brother, Richard, who died tragically in a car wreck at age twenty, were raised in that house.

Mamie, who died of a heart attack when I was seven, first awakened my love of music. I recall sitting next to her as she tickled the ivories—and they were *ivories*—on the upright piano in the sitting room. "What shall we sing today?" she'd ask, but the question was purely rhetorical, since we always started with nursery songs, *London Bridge is Falling Down*, *Rock-a-bye Baby*, and naturally, *Old MacDonald Had a Farm*, which allowed me to cluck, grunt, and moo to my heart's content.

When I saw Mamie reach for the tattered and worn Methodist hymnal, I braced myself for some serious singing: *Holy, Holy, Holy*, *Love Divine All Loves Excelling*, and *All Hail the Power of Jesus' Name*. I waited eagerly for our grand finale—my favorite—*Come Thou Fount of Every Blessing*. I knew every word of it from memory, although it would be many years before I had any inkling what the text actually meant.

Both Mamie and Gran told me stories about my Uncle Richard, who had played first-chair clarinet in the school band. How I wished that he were still alive, so he could participate in Mamie's and my music-making.

Gran's sunny, congenial presence graced my life throughout my childhood and early adult years. On Sundays, he got "gussied up" (his term) in a suit and tie for Sunday school and church. Monday through Saturday, he donned his faded blue overalls and old straw hat and headed out for the fields or the barnyard. Gran found contentment and joy in working the land; part of his soul was in the soil that he plowed. His rough, calloused hands revealed a life of continuous labor, yet these same hands were frequently outstretched, kindly and gently, to help a neighbor or pat me on the cheek. He totally won my heart when he made a beautiful wooden cradle for my dolls.

I am pictured with Granddaddy Covington.
Gran is holding the metal bar connecting my legs.

Gran saw the humor in almost any situation. He often recounted a story about going to the hospital as a young man to have his gallbladder removed (in those days, a major operation). His nurse had explained that he couldn't go home until he passed gas: "Don't you know, Mr. Covington, that every time you pass gas, it's a feather in my cap?" Gran responded, "Well, stand back, lady, because I'm about to make you an Indian chief!"

Gran enjoyed nothing more than spinning a good yarn, particularly when it involved his daddy, William Jennings Covington, who, for obscure reasons, had been called "Cooge" (rhymes with "Scrooge"). Cooge had a talent for devising shrewd, if not downright devious, ways of earning extra money. Whenever he took his horse and buggy to town, there'd be a sign on the back: LUNGS TESTED—5 CENTS. Usually, at least one unsuspecting soul would take the bait: "Cooge, I'd like to have my lungs tested."

Pocketing the nickel first, Cooge would chuckle: "Sure—it's

7

easy. Just lift up my old nag's tail and blow as hard as you can. If the bit falls out of her mouth, your lungs are in fine shape!" Daddy sometimes jokingly accused Gran of exaggerating Cooge's exploits, but I believed Gran when he said it was The Gospel Truth.

When, in 1950, my parents and I moved into our new brick bungalow a quarter-mile down the highway, I instantly felt the coziness and warmth of home. In the years ahead—after my schooling and career took me hundreds of miles away—I could conjure up, at a moment's notice, feelings of safety, security, and belonging, simply by thinking of that modest house built on what had once been a cotton field.

DADDY POSSESSED MANY STERLING QUALITIES: unshakable integrity, high moral standards, a strong work ethic, concern for neighbors and friends, dedication to church and community— and he had drop-dead gorgeous blue eyes.

Having inherited his mother's deeply introspective, intensely private temperament, Daddy was not the easiest person to know or understand. He seldom divulged his inner thoughts; and even when he appeared to be revealing himself, I always suspected that he wasn't telling me everything. In our sixty-four years as father and daughter, we shared remarkably few confidences. I sometimes wished that Daddy were more like Gran, whose heart was an open book.

Daddy epitomized the strong, silent type. I cherish those all-too-rare occasions when he openly displayed affection and approval. At my high school graduation ceremony, as the class president pushed me up the aisle of the auditorium in my wheelchair, I caught Daddy's eye. He flashed me a smile and a wink—and I can still feel the surge of warmth and joy that engulfed my whole body at that moment.

No man ever worked harder than Daddy to provide for his family. As a child, I was keenly aware that the pressures and uncertainties of farming weighed heavily on his shoulders. Every year, he made dire predictions about rainfall shortages, crop failures, and financial ruin. I eventually disregarded these prophecies, since they never came true, at least not to the extent I had expected.

As an adult, I had a closer, more relaxed relationship with Daddy. (Perhaps we both grew up.) During the years that Mother had Alzheimer's, he and I bonded in a common concern for her. Toward the end of his life, Daddy became more mellow and jovial like Gran.

ON APRIL 13, 1951, I BECAME A PROUD "BIG SISTER" to Mary Jo—a beautiful, healthy, able-bodied baby. I had anticipated playing with her as I did my dolls, but I discovered she was much too big and wiggly for that. As children, we had little in common due to the difference in our ages, but as adults, we became close friends. Growing up with me as an older sibling was undoubtedly difficult, because Mother and Daddy were frequently preoccupied with my physical problems. Whatever Mary Jo's frustrations may have been, she never allowed them to affect our relationship. I could not have asked for a more loving, loyal sister. In 2006, she proved her mettle by saving me from a life-threatening illness. *Every day*, I give thanks that I am not an only child.

MY SECOND HIP SURGERY, scheduled for the fall of 1952, almost delayed the start of my schooling, since a waist-high cast would have made it impossible for me to sit at a desk in a regular classroom. However, in August, Mother and Daddy learned that Mrs. Janet Carlisle, a veteran public school teacher, was choosing six boys and six girls for a private first-grade class at her home in

Bennettsville. The timing couldn't have been more perfect. Mother explained my situation to Mrs. Carlisle, who readily agreed that I could prop up on her living room couch during my weeks in a cast.

My remaining surgeries took place in the summer, so I attended the Bennettsville public schools, beginning with the second grade. At this point, I became more conscious of my disability. Although in those days, I could walk with support, I was still different from the mass of other children. I did not go outside for recess in cold weather (I couldn't run around and keep warm), and Mother or my teacher had to help me to the bathroom during the lunch break. These physical constraints were not pleasant and certainly not what I would have chosen for myself, but neither were they onerous or unbearable. No one made fun of me or treated me unkindly.

My second grade teacher *was* guilty of an unfortunate incident of thoughtlessness. One day, when the alarm sounded for a fire drill, everyone left the room and forgot about me! Alone and frightened, I envisioned the building going up in flames. In my panic, I even began to smell smoke. A few minutes later, the teacher and students returned to find me screaming hysterically. Of course, my teacher felt horrible. Apologizing profusely, she called Mother to explain what had happened. Mother came to the school, and I gradually regained my composure. From then on, the principal always told me in advance when fire drills would take place. Sworn to secrecy, I could tell no one, not even my teacher. Having this privileged information made me feel quite special and important.

MY FIRST VOCAL PERFORMANCE, at the tender age of six, took everyone by surprise. My Sunday school class was being given a tour of the church sanctuary. When we entered the choir loft, the teacher asked if anyone would like to sing a solo. As if I'd been waiting for my big chance, I unhesitatingly volunteered a rousing rendition of the *Battle Hymn of the Republic.*

Upon hearing what I had done, and perhaps recalling the story of the baby bird, Mother asked our church organist, Faye Griggs, to teach me a song that would be suitable as a church solo. Within a year, I had sung *The Lord's Prayer* not only in church, but also in a local talent contest, where I won second prize. My award was a grand total of three dollars!

Mother began to wonder if I might be physically capable of

Here I am (second from left) with the other winners of the talent contest. I was relying on the man behind me (the school's principal, I believe) for balance and support.

playing a musical instrument. She again consulted Faye Griggs, who happened to be one of Bennettsville's most respected piano teachers. They agreed that I would begin lessons in the fall of 1954. Why did Mother encourage me to play the piano? It seems a rather startling, even audacious course of action, given the severity of my physical problems, especially the malformation of my right wrist. The answer, I think, lies in the simple fact that she saw my musical potential and wanted to help me realize that potential in every possible way. Knowingly or not, she put me on a path that led eventually to a satisfying, successful career. Even more important, she allowed me to discover for myself that my disability need not impede my hopes and dreams, that my happiness lay in focusing on my assets, not my limitations.

My maternal grandfather Bunyan Bailey ("B.B.") Benfield built and operated the first movie theater in Dillon, South Carolina, in the 1920s. In 1936, upon learning that a competitor would soon enter the market and realizing Dillon could not support two theaters, B.B. took the seemingly risky step of moving to the fledgling community of Myrtle Beach, building the first two theaters there. He lived to see a hefty return on his investment when Myrtle Beach became a booming metropolis and tourist attraction.

******

After Daddy retired from farming, his vegetable garden continued to produce the crispiest corn, the juiciest tomatoes, the most gargantuan collards, and the sweetest "sweet taters" in the county. In his later years, he planted only the "Covington" sweet potato, named for his cousin, horticulturalist Henry M. Covington.

SWEET POTATO KEEPS NATIVE'S MEMORY ALIVE
By Lynn McQueen
(From the *Marlboro Herald-Advocate*, Bennettsville, S.C.)

Harry Covington, retired farmer and avid gardener, thinks he just may have found the perfect sweet potato.

It's plump and tasty and so sweet that it doesn't need sugar. What's more, it's a sentimental favorite, named the "Covington" after his late cousin Henry.

Both men were born and raised near Bennettsville. They were actually closer than first cousins; their fathers were double first cousins, and their mothers were sisters.

Harry has retired from farming but still maintains a large garden near his home on Highway 9 East; Henry lived in Apex, N.C., and died in 2004 at age 89.

The "Covington" was the first new sweet potato variety to be developed in North Carolina in many years. Henry didn't develop it, but he was widely considered to be a sweet potato expert and is credited with helping build the sweet potato industry in North Carolina.

He worked as a horticulture professor at N.C. State University from 1948 to 1973, earning numerous honors, including Outstanding Extension Horticulturalist in the United States and awards from the N.C. Yam Commission and Certified Sweet Potato Seed Growers Program. He also is credited with starting the N.C. Sweet Potato Commission and the U.S. Sweet Potato Council.

It was because of that background, which spanned 50 years of service to farmers, that the N.C. Sweet Potato Commission decided to name the new sweet potato in his honor last year.

Covington died in October 2004, before the potato could be named. But family members said he was told of the decision in his last days and was touched.

This was the first year that the "Covington" was available to producers. The variety made up half of Harry's sweet potato crop, which he's harvesting now, and he's so pleased with the outcome that he plans to grow only the "Covington" next year.

"It's definitely better than other sweet potatoes," he said with a smile. "Of course, I take a little credit for that, too. I quit farming but I raise a right good bit of produce to give away. I always say my garden is where the Garden of Eden used to be."

******

A WARTIME ROMANCE

I suspect that my parents' romance was typical of many couples of their day. They met as sophomores at Furman University in Greenville, South Carolina, and soon found themselves going steady. According to Mother's diary, by their senior year, they were happily in love and had discussed marriage. The entry of May 19, 1940, is particularly charming: "Dated Harry tonight. Sat on rock under campus tree." No doubt, holding hands and smooching.

Mother and Daddy were creditable students in their respective curricula—English and business—but neither would have been considered an "intellectual." Based on Mother's diary, I picture them as a "power couple," influential in many circles, participating and excelling in a wide range of activities: social, scholastic, athletic, and recreational. Daddy's leadership abilities, not to mention his movie-star good looks, propelled him to president of the student council his senior year. Mother, who had been an avid tennis player since the age of twelve, was dismayed to discover that Furman had no tennis team for women, so she and a group of her friends sprang into action and organized one. This accomplishment would eventually earn Mother a place in the Furman Athletic Hall of Fame.

"Courting days." Christine Benfield and Harry Covington on the tennis court at Furman University, Greenville, S.C., ca. 1939.

About a year after their graduation in the spring of 1940, Mother received her engagement ring and Daddy his commission in the Navy. World War II had begun, and Daddy, like many young men at that time, felt a moral as well as a patriotic obligation to serve in the military. He was assigned to a transport ship in the North Atlantic where German submarines were a constant threat. Daddy liked to recall that although the only weapons they had were handguns, his ingenious skipper asked a carpenter on board to build a wooden profile of a gun and mount it on the ship's deck to fool the German submarines. The ship made it safely back to New York by running a zigzag course and keeping the lights off.

At first, it seemed best to postpone marriage until the war ended. However, on October 23, 1942, Daddy called Mother, who was teaching fifth grade in Myrtle Beach, and said, "Uncle Sam is giving me some time off; let's get married *tomorrow*!" And so their leisurely four-year courtship ended with a spur-of-the-moment wedding on a three-day pass.

After being transferred to an amphibious unit in the Pacific, Daddy participated in six invasions in seventeen months. During this period, Mother lived in California. She applied for a job at a factory that made parachutes for U.S. troops; she was hired, but only after undergoing an extensive background check and submitting many letters of recommendation. One day, her supervisor approached her, complimented her on her work, and told her he had never seen credentials more stellar than hers. In retrospect, she understood the necessity of security precautions, considering the vital role of parachutes in the war effort. Mother also kept herself busy playing tennis and spending time with Daddy's Aunt Lucy and Uncle John D. Smith (Grandmother Covington's younger brother) and their daughter, Patricia, who lived near San Francisco. Of course, she saw Daddy whenever he was on leave; I was conceived during one of his onshore visits.

After the war, they made their home in Bennettsville with my Covington grandparents. Daddy began his farming career with Gran, and Mother prepared to give birth to me.

THE DANCE OF DISCIPLINE

PIANO PLAYING provided the ideal focus for my energy and creativity—a way of escaping, literally and metaphorically, the confines of my physical disability. Up to that point, my right hand had been utterly useless. With my wrist locked in its congenital position, I couldn't hold a spoon, pick up a toy, or comb my dolls' hair. I had been, in effect, one-handed. However, I could press down a piano key with my right fingers; I could make interesting, beautiful sounds at the keyboard with both hands. Throughout my pianistic career, that sense of accomplishment, that sense of release from my limitations, sustained and nourished me, physically and spiritually.

With her characteristic efficiency and superb organizational skills, Mother had devised a rigorous schedule for my daily practicing. On weekday mornings, she woke me up at 6:00 a.m. sharp, so that I could have an hour at the piano before going to school. Since, unlike Mother, I was not by nature an early riser, I initially balked at this plan. To make matters worse, Mother insisted that I eat a hearty breakfast. Sometimes I actually fell asleep with food in my mouth. Of course, Mother's tough love prevailed, and my resentment rapidly declined with the realization that morning practicing left my afternoons free for homework and other activities. For the next fifteen years—through grammar school, high school, and college—this routine served me well.

I am immensely grateful for Mother's instinctive understanding that discipline is an essential survival skill for the disabled. When the simplest tasks require assistance and concerted effort, a strong work ethic and a healthy acceptance of one's limitations can make the crucial difference between a "good" life and a life of frustration and misery.

I no longer rise at six in the morning, but I still tend to be a disciplined, regimented person and prefer to accomplish difficult tasks early in the day. While I sometimes envy my more spontaneous friends, I've found that, for me, the best way to get things done is to set up a schedule and stick to it.

I don't know how I played the piano that first year with my rigid right wrist; I do know that Faye Griggs's enthusiasm, optimism, wisdom, and musicality made her the perfect teacher for me.

The charming little pieces of the Bernice Frost method books presented the basics of note-reading and rhythm, though almost immediately, Faye began supplementing this material with sheet music solos. Twice a year, Faye presented her students in recital at the grammar school auditorium—the same stage where I had won second prize in the talent contest. I eagerly awaited my pianistic debut as I memorized *Skylark*, four pages of hand-over-hand repetitive patterns encompassing the entire range of the keyboard. Playing this "big piece" successfully for an audience sent my spirits soaring and solidified my resolve to continue piano study.

Faye agreed that I had made excellent progress but urged Mother and Daddy to investigate the possibility of my having corrective surgery. As we drove to Charlotte to see Dr. Jacobs, my stomach was in knots. However, I perked up when he assured us that the removal of extra bones and tissue from beneath my right wrist would enhance flexibility and allow for a more normal hand position at the piano. Mother spoke glowingly of my recent recital performance. Turning to me, Dr. Jacobs said, "After we fix your wrist, you'll play even better, faster, and stronger." I responded without hesitation, "Let's do it!"

The night before my surgery, Mother and I had settled in at the hospital. I tried to maintain a brave front, but inside, my feelings vacillated between frustration and anguish. Why did my life have to be so complicated? Why did I have to go under the knife, when most piano students improve their technique simply by practicing more scales with the metronome? What if the surgery failed? What if even my limited pianistic abilities were taken away?

I asked Mother to take me to the piano that was located in one of the hospital's public areas. As I began playing one of my favorite pieces, *The Wedding of the Dolls*, Dr. Jacobs spotted us. He came over to me, gave me a hug, and said, "Don't worry, Vickie. After tomorrow, you'll be able to play even better with your new wrist."

Dr. Jacobs never heard me play the piano again, but his prediction came true. The procedure of June 1955 is the only one of my childhood operations that I can honestly say yielded positive results; it made possible the next thirty years of pianistic achievement. Of course, the surgery also gave me a more functional right hand for everyday living. And when the use of a manual wheelchair became necessary, the ability to propel myself with both hands was of crucial significance.

MY MUSICAL HORIZONS EXPANDED RAPIDLY as Faye introduced me to legitimate piano literature—the lively sonatinas of Haydn and Clementi as well as more lyrical pieces from Schumann's *Album for the Young*. Concerns about my pedal technique vanished when I discovered that I could use my strong, dependable *left* foot.

Faye frequently played the organ works of J.S. Bach in our church on Sunday, so I was thrilled to discover that Bach had also written music for piano. I found the pieces of the *Anna Magdalena Notebook* and *Little Preludes* both pianistically challenging and artistically rewarding. My crowning achievement came when I learned Bach's *Two-Part Invention in F Major*. I remember analyzing this little masterpiece with Faye, going measure by measure, seeing how the theme moves back and forth between the hands. I can still conjure up the exhilaration I felt as I played that piece securely from memory.

Except for my hand position, which was never completely normal, Faye held me to the same rigorous standards that she set for her other students. She provided a solid foundation in every aspect of musicianship, including music theory. In a seemingly never-ending series of "Theory Papers," I studied scales, chords, intervals, musical terms and symbols. These exercises, though not as enjoyable as playing "real music," proved to be indispensable to my future development as a professional musician.

In my third year of study, I had the opportunity to put my pianistic skills to practical use. The Men's Bible Class at First United Methodist Church needed an accompanist. Since both Daddy and Gran were class members, I didn't have to be asked twice. The song leader for the class informed me up-front that in certain hymns, the men liked to take liberties with the music—slowing down or speeding up the tempo. It would be my job to listen for these nuances and adapt my playing accordingly. By the time I relinquished the position ten years later, not only could I sight-read the entire *Cokesbury Hymnal*—I had become a sensitive, musically alert accompanist. To this day, I can tell you that *What a Friend We Have in Jesus* is in the key of F Major, and upon request, I will gladly sing all three verses.

When I presented my senior piano recital at St. Andrews College, the Men's Bible Class turned out *en masse* to support me, and before I left for graduate school, they gave me a large, sturdy suitcase that went with me on my travels for the next twenty-five years. Whenever I packed or unpacked that bag, I recalled what a privilege it had been to grow up under the watchful eye of a whole bevy of surrogate grandfathers and Dutch uncles.

THROUGHOUT MY CHILDHOOD, my girlfriends and I took turns going to each other's houses on Saturday to spend the day. My favorite pastime was playing with dolls, followed (a close second) by playing "dress-up" and "movie star." The latter combined the best elements of the other pastimes; I felt like a living doll, dressed in glamorous garb, as I invariably assumed the role of Doris Day. Mother took me to see many of her films. Her looks, her clothes, her personality, and her singing voice sent me into flights of rapture. Best of all, her adventures, as depicted on the big screen, always ended happily; I wanted my life to be just like hers.

I never completely recovered from my crush on Doris Day. Years later, when Mother and I went shopping to choose evening gowns for my piano concerts, I'd laughingly say, "Well, I guess I'm still playing dress-up" or "I wonder what Doris would think of this color."

Putting it mildly, I have always been a girly-girl. Clothes and jewelry were—and are—among my greatest passions. Every Halloween, Mother asked me what kind of costume I wanted. Every year I said I wanted to be a gypsy, because that meant I could wear a brightly colored outfit and lots of jewelry.

A STRICT UPBRINGING forged my tough character and resilient spirit. In our household, rules were enforced with complete consistency. My parents tolerated no complaining, no sassy talk, and positively no whining.

How envious I felt when some of my classmates told me they actually received monetary rewards for good grades. I couldn't believe it. My "all-A" report cards were met with tacit approval; the presence of even one "B" elicited a lecture about "working harder and doing better next time." Ironically, on my very first report card, I received a "B" in conduct, because I socialized too much in class. Warnings of a possible "B" hadn't fazed me, since I didn't know what a report card was. Needless to say, my parents made me see the error of my ways. Eventually, Mother confided that she and Daddy had secretly smiled over that "B." After all, I had been raised in the country with limited access to children my own age. When given the opportunity to interact with my peers, I understandably got a bit carried away.

My biggest disappointment in elementary school came with my assignment to the third-grade class of Miss Bedenbaugh—a lean, lanky tyrant with the type of horn-rimmed glasses and a perennial frown that have become cliché for instructors of her era. I had desperately hoped for Mrs. McLeod, who was beloved by all her students. Upon learning my fate, I burst into tears. Did Mother and Daddy intervene to have me transferred to Mrs. McLeod's class? No way. They admonished me to shape up. "Miss Bedenbaugh is your teacher, and there is much you can learn from her. Life doesn't always give you what you will want. You'll just have to make the best of it. Period."

Like my assignment to Miss Bedenbaugh's class, my disability was simply a fact of life. I was expected to do everything I could do to the best of my ability; we wasted no time worrying about things I couldn't do.

Writing "thank-you" notes comprised an essential part of my upbringing. My orthopedic surgeries prompted many relatives and friends to send me cards and gifts. From the beginning, Mother made sure that I sent a token of thanks to each person.

Before I could write, I drew or colored a picture. As soon as I learned to print the alphabet, Mother would draft a note, which I meticulously copied. Mother's notes were models of graciousness, and by the age of eleven or twelve, I could express myself easily and confidently. I began composing my own notes, not mailing them, however, until they passed Mother's inspection. Upon reaching high school, I took sole responsibility for my correspondence, only occasionally asking Mother's advice.

Response to my notes surprised me; compliments poured in. Obviously, receiving a well expressed, heartfelt "thank you" enhanced the joy of giving. Soon Mother began encouraging me to send sympathy cards, get well messages, and other kinds of notes. Although I sometimes selected printed cards, I always added a sentence or two of my own.

Faced with the ordeals of orthopedic surgery and the daily challenges of being physically disabled, I could easily have spent my life feeling sorry for myself. Instead, from my earliest years, Mother systematically and matter-of-factly directed my attention to the kindness and thoughtfulness of others.

Mother followed the same training procedure with Mary Jo, who once remarked, "Vickie, you and I may not be aware of every rule of social etiquette, but, by golly, we can write a decent 'thank-you' note!"

FOLLOWING SOUTHERN TRADITION, my parents allowed Mary Jo and me to call adult friends by their first names, provided the name was preceded by "Miss" or "Mister." In our part of the country, this is considered an appropriate combination of familiarity and respect.

I had no problem until I encountered the Southern penchant for assigning people bizarre nicknames. Mother had two childhood friends called "Piggy" and "Teeny." Daddy had male friends—fine, upstanding members of the community—known as "Punk," "Bumsey," "Skeet," and "Ubba." In the case of the man who used to mow Daddy's lawn, we knew only that the nickname sounded like "Bootie." Seeking enlightenment, I asked Daddy, "Are you saying 'Boo-Dee' or 'Boo-Tee' and what does it mean?" His response: "I have no idea."

Surely I'm not the only child who has ever cringed at the thought of saying "Miss Piggy" and "Mister Punk." I finally gave up and decided just to smile and say, "Hi." Now that I am (somewhat reluctantly) on the receiving end of this familial respect, I am incredibly grateful that my parents gave me a respectable, honorable nickname I can live with.

MOTHER'S STRONG SENSE OF DISCIPLINE did not preclude her enjoyment of life's pleasures—like eating dessert. Although she professed a dislike for cooking, she furnished a steady supply of savory goodies: pecan pie, lemon meringue pie, made-from-scratch cake with chocolate sauce (served warm), butterscotch brownies, and old-fashioned teacakes. No wonder I still consider it a sin of omission to end a meal without "a little taste of something sweet."

DADDY BOUGHT OUR FIRST TV when I was about ten. With only "rabbit ears" for an antenna, we could get exactly two channels, CBS and NBC. I became absorbed in the afternoon soap operas. When the main character on *The Edge of Night* (a police detective, as I recall) lost his wife to some terrible illness, I literally wept. In later years, I was glued to the musical/variety shows of Perry Como and Andy Williams.

Once I progressed beyond mindless, fluffy entertainment, TV introduced me to a lifelong passion, as I began to follow religiously thoroughbred racing's Triple Crown: the Kentucky Derby, Preakness, and Belmont Stakes. I learned the facts and figures of the favorites, then waited to see if one of them would win. Every year, I hoped for a Triple Crown Champion. (My all-time favorite is Secretariat.) I am still an avid fan of these races. I not only watch them on TV, but also record them, so I can replay the most exciting, or most distressing, moments. And no, I have never placed a single bet!

Figure skating enthralled me because of its close association with music and dance, not to mention those glamorous costumes. As a special treat, Mother and Daddy took me to Charlotte, North Carolina, several times to see the Ice Capades. TV has allowed me to follow the careers of all the great skaters through the years. Had I been able-bodied, there is no doubt in my mind that I would have tried to master this artistic sport. To some extent, I envied the exploits of figure skaters and other athletes, yet I never felt deprived or cheated; I had found my spotlight in music.

IN AUGUST 1957, Gran took his second wife, Nettie Gibson, a retired elementary schoolteacher who had never been married. "Miss Nettie" wasted no time settling into her new role as step-grandmother to Mary Jo and me. We loved her dearly and thrived on the attention. In the summer of 1958, when I had my final right hip surgery, Miss Nettie gave me a whole bag of presents to take with me to the hospital (one to open each day).

A few weeks prior to that surgery, I attended a birthday dance for one of my classmates. Decked out in my favorite party dress, I "slow-danced" with six or eight different boys, sometimes changing partners during a dance. (Mother said it was called "cutting in.") For days afterward, I relived the magical memories of that night . . . the feeling of holding my partner's hand, his arm around my waist, my arm resting on his shoulder. In those fleeting moments, my Doris Day fantasies had come to life.

My upcoming surgery made me feel vaguely uneasy. Physically,

I was doing extremely well. I had even danced! Perhaps, I thought, it would be wise to "leave well enough alone." I wish now that I had voiced my misgivings, but would anyone have taken seriously the opinion of a twelve-year-old?

The surgery was a failure. *I never danced again.*

Since, from day one, Dr. Jacobs freely admitted that in all his experience, he had never encountered a muscular-skeletal system exactly like mine, I now regard my childhood surgeries as being largely experimental. I am convinced that my last surgery set me on a course that led ultimately to my dependence on a wheelchair.

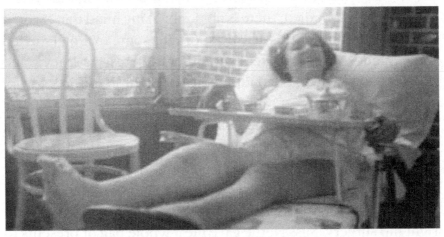

Summer 1958: I had a special lounge chair on our enclosed porch where I spent my days recuperating from my final hip surgery.

In the aftermath of that failed surgery, I confronted the fact that my disability would likely be permanent. There would be no magic cures, no quick fixes. Not now. Not ever. With a heavy heart, I pondered the possibility that if I lived for a long time, I'd have to cope with my physical limitations for seemingly countless years. These were sobering thoughts for a twelve-year-old.

On the other hand, I felt extremely grateful that my condition was stable and painless. In Dr. Jacobs's waiting room, I had observed many children who suffered from deformities infinitely more severe than mine. I quickly concluded that I should count my blessings and stop worrying about the future.

My spirits received an additional, unexpected boost when Dr. Jacobs decided to release me from his care. For the first time, I felt free—free to live my life in my own way. The traumatic hospitalizations, the nauseating ether, and the long weeks of confinement in a cast would become distant memories. At last, I could put my disability where it belonged, on the sideline, and concentrate on schoolwork, family, friends, and music.

FAYE GRIGGS'S DEPARTURE from Bennettsville in 1960 to accept a church organist position in Oak Ridge, Tennessee, left me devastated. She had secured my musical future, however, by arranging for me to study with another Fay—Fay McLaurin—a piano graduate of Winthrop College in Rock Hill, South Carolina, whom I had adored as my public school music teacher in the fourth grade.

My lessons with Fay had scarcely begun when a tragic occurrence thrust me into the spotlight at First United Methodist Church. One Sunday morning, the young man who had recently been hired as organist (replacing Faye Griggs) died in a car wreck on his way to church. I remember vividly someone coming into the Men's Bible Class, giving me the awful news, and immediately asking me if I would play the piano for the 11:00 a.m. service. I had no choice but to jump in and do the best I could. For the next six weeks, I served as church pianist, until a replacement organist could be found. At fourteen, I was undoubtedly the youngest person ever to hold the job.

In this crisis Fay McLaurin proved to be indispensable. She selected appropriate pieces for me to play as preludes, offertories, and postludes, and coached me in accompaniment techniques for congregational singing. My spur-of-the-moment performance that first Sunday had been timid and tentative, but by the sixth week, with Fay's help, I was well on my way to being a poised professional. And the enthusiastic support of the church members further enhanced my confidence.

During my high school years (1960-64), under Fay's expert guidance, I broadened my repertoire, expanded my technique, and honed my artistry at the keyboard. As I studied several lovely, romantic pieces from Felix Mendelssohn's *Songs Without Words*, we spent many lessons on the concept of *tempo rubato*, the subtle give-and-take of tempo that is the life's blood of nineteenth-century music. She insisted that the melody lines be smooth (*legato*), singing (*cantabile*), and properly balanced with the accompaniment. I learned more Bach *Two-Part Inventions*, which I had to memorize "hands separately" with correct fingering, articulation, and dynamic contrasts. This strategy, I discovered, made the playing of these pieces "hands together" much easier. For the first time, piano music of the twentieth century became part of my repertoire: Debussy's *First Arabesque*, Jacques Ibert's *The Little White Donkey*, and George Frederick McKay's *Excursion*.

At the piano I regarded my disability as little more than an inconvenience. Even after I began to rely on a wheelchair for mobility, I could stand and transfer to the piano bench without assistance. I continued to use my strong, steady left foot for the damper (sustaining) pedal. Although my right hand spanned only a seventh and my left hand barely an octave, Fay and I found no shortage of musically interesting repertoire that I could play comfortably and convincingly.

Technical difficulties at the keyboard were solved through adaptation, adjustment, ingenuity, and common sense. On the surface, these strategies might seem mutually exclusive, even contradictory. However, from my earliest years, I had the good fortune to work with teachers who understood—and helped me to understand—that the best approach to problem-solving combines idealism and pragmatism, hope and reason, creativity and discipline.

At first I relied on Fay to analyze my technical problems and suggest solutions, although I eventually became almost totally independent as I experimented with a variety of unorthodox techniques: unusual fingerings, playing notes with the left hand that would ordinarily be played with the right (and vice versa), and even an occasional bit of "editing," such as omitting the upper or lower notes of octaves, provided the integrity of the music was not jeopardized. My playing proved that a performer can effectively communicate the musical content of a piece without playing every note exactly as it appears on the printed page. I can state unequivocally that a pianist's most important assets are good ears and a good mind—not nimble fingers.

Both Faye Griggs and Fay McLaurin were vivacious, charming, fun-loving women—but in appearance and teaching style, they could hardly have been more different.

Faye Griggs had a short, stocky frame. She generally greeted me at my lessons wearing a coordinated skirt and blouse with an eye-catching necklace. She sat in a straight chair, quite near the piano, taking copious notes as I played. Only occasionally did she stop me in the middle of a piece to make a comment. Her sug-gestions tended to be straightforward and to-the-point.

Tall and thin, Fay McLaurin tended to dress for comfort, usually slacks and a pullover sweater. During my lessons, she wandered around the room, watching and listening to me from different vantage points. Sometimes she draped her long limbs over an easy chair on the far side of the room, a mug of coffee nearby. She often spoke in descriptive imagery and routinely interrupted my playing in order to make a comment that "couldn't wait."

I would not have changed a single thing about either of them; I cherished their similarities as well as their differences. Together, they imparted the knowledge and helped me develop the skills that were absolutely essential for my musical career. *I never had to unlearn anything they taught me.*

I HAD ENJOYED A RELATIVELY NORMAL SOCIAL LIFE as a child; however, as an adolescent, I felt socially isolated—no dates, no proms, no boyfriends. Although boys were friendly and polite to me, I think they were intimidated by my disability. I was bitterly disappointed to be "missing out" on an important rite of passage. Rerunning all those Doris Day movies in my mind, I imagined myself at a grand ball, being relentlessly pursued by hordes of handsome men, all of whom wanted to dance with me. I invariably chose the handsomest candidate, who whisked me onto the ballroom floor, then off to happily-ever-after land. As thrilling as these fantasies were, I would gladly have traded them for just one honest-to-goodness, real-life romance.

Would I have had a more active social life if I had been able-bodied? Perhaps, though in retrospect, I suspect that boys may have found my single-minded focus on music and academia equally as daunting as my disability. In any event, homework and practicing provided solace and refuge—a convenient escape from life's disappointments. The piano remained my first love, and by the age of sixteen, I had made the decision to be a performance major in college.

Without a doubt, my disability facilitated my academic achievement. Having few social distractions, I could indulge fully my genuine enjoyment of reading and studying. Good grades were the natural result.

English became my favorite academic subject in the seventh grade, when my teacher, Mr. L.E. Smith, awed me with his command of the language. He left no noun unmodified, no verb unconjugated. The intricacies of grammar fascinated me; from that point on, I enjoyed manipulating words.

At age twelve, I began to write short poems. My efforts were hardly profound, but I had fun experimenting with different meters and rhyme schemes. I submitted "God Speaks To Me" to a Methodist magazine for young people, *Trails for Juniors*, never expecting it to be published. I felt positively jubilant when the next issue arrived, and I saw my words in print. Another of my poems, "Assurance," written for a high school English assignment, was published in the school's literary magazine.

In my sophomore year, I entered the high school declamation contest, performing "Betty at the Baseball Game," an hilarious monologue about an airhead who thinks "catching a fly" refers to an insect and "stealing bases" is an act of thievery. I didn't win— I didn't even make the finals—but the enthusiastic response of the audience made me contemplate, briefly, a career in acting.

When my eleventh-grade English teacher required every student to make a speech to the class (on any topic we chose), I decided to combine my musical and verbal skills by preparing an overview of art, literature, and music in the Baroque, Classical, Romantic, and Contemporary styles. That day, the class met in the auditorium, where the grand piano was located. I showed paintings, read poetry, and played piano pieces to illustrate each period, all within about thirty minutes. My teacher and classmates seemed stunned by the scope of my presentation; those students who had not yet made their speeches said I'd be a tough act to follow. No one accused me of not being ambitious. In fact, I think that performance clinched my image as an over-achiever.

PUTTING ALL MY EGGS IN ONE BASKET, I applied for admission only at St. Andrews Presbyterian College (now St. Andrews University) in Laurinburg, North Carolina. The school seemed an ideal choice for me because of its new physically accessible campus, its excellent music department, and its proximity to Bennettsville (only twelve miles from my parents' home). Fay had complete faith in my ability, but would the St. Andrews music faculty accept someone with my physical limitations into the Bachelor of Music degree program as a piano performance major?

My audition in the spring of 1964 was a triumph. Fay and I had chosen repertoire that showcased my musical prowess and minimized my technical deficiencies. She had drilled me thoroughly in scales, chords, and other aspects of music theory. That day, I even managed to sight-read decently. I was accepted on the spot. Years later, the St. Andrews organ professor told Mother that he had never heard a stronger, more "musical" audition performance.

THE HIGHLIGHT OF MY SENIOR YEAR came when I presented a piano recital in the Bennettsville High School auditorium—a delightful occasion attended by about one hundred family members and friends. The modest program included solo pieces as well as several duets with Fay. For the first time, I did not have to share the stage with other students, and I loved every minute of it.

As graduation approached, I learned that I was class valedictorian and that I would receive a special award for being the student with the highest cumulative average in English. Weeks earlier, I had agreed to sing a solo at the commencement ceremonies; Fay and I had selected *Let There Be Peace On Earth (And Let It Begin With Me)*, a relatively new song at that time.

My duties as valedictorian included making a speech; not wanting to monopolize the spotlight, I quickly and easily made the choice to sing, passing the speech to the salutatorian. Though confident of my verbal skills, I preferred, as usual, to express myself musically. With the passage of many years, the salutatorian's speech has probably long since been forgotten, but, given music's power to capture and communicate the emotional significance of an occasion, I'm reasonably sure that at least a few of my classmates still remember my vocal solo.

GOD SPEAKS TO ME

God speaks to me sometimes while I am on a mountain high,
And sometimes while watching breathlessly a sunset in the sky,
Or very often when I see a fluffy cloud go by.

God speaks to me each time I see a jagged lightning bolt,
And when I hear a thunderclap reply in bold revolt,
Or when I see a mother horse standing o'er her newborn colt.

Each time I see a rocket taking off for outer space,
I thank God for the knowledge that he gave the human race,
But pray that it will not bring to us a third world war to face.

Each time I see the ocean I can hear God speak to me,
Or when I see a hero's grave, which recalls the memory
That he gave his life that we might live in a country strong and
free.

God does not only speak to me in moonlit lakes and bays;
He also speaks to everyone in nature's wondrous ways,
Which reminds us that His holy presence ever with us stays!

ASSURANCE

Sometimes when all the world seems full of gloom,
And pressures rise around me everywhere,
Within my heart there seems to be no room
For the cheerfulness and love that should be there.

Each little problem then appears to grow,
And my hopes get still slimmer every day.
I ask, "Where is the peace I used to know?
Where are those carefree days, so light and gay?"

Yet just when life is but a pathless maze
And all the roads ahead are black as night,
Slowly appears a lifting of the haze,
And through the dark I see a ray of light.

I hear the voice of God speak to my soul,
Saying that all these trials will pass in time,
That He will stay to guide me through the whole
Of life, if I but trust His will divine.

Now every care begins to disappear,
And all the worry from my mind is gone.
Divine assurance makes the future clear,
For I am sure I'll never walk alone.

SENIOR HIGH SCHOOL RECITAL

Bennettsville High School Auditorium
Bennettsville, S.C.
June 4, 1964

The Cuckoo and the Nightingale (Duet) .... Handel
Arioso ....Bach
Finale from Sonatina in C Major .... Haydn
La Campanella (Duet) .... Liszt

Boat Song in G Minor .... Mendelssohn
Boat Song in A Major .... Mendelssohn
Chopin (from "Carnival") .... Schumann

The Arrogant Rooster and the Humble Hen .... Fischer
Excursion .... McKay
The Little White Donkey ....Ibert
Jamaican Rhumba (Duet) ....Benjamin

Fantasia on "Greensleeves" (Duet) .... Vaughan Williams
First Arabesque .... Debussy
Clair de Lune .... Debussy
Valse (Duet) .... Rachmaninoff

All duets were played with my teacher, Fay McLaurin.

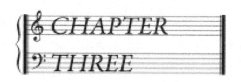

CHAPTER THREE

THE VERACITY OF THE ZOROASTRIAN

UNLIKE MANY TEENAGERS, who assert their independence by "going off to college," I remained in the familial nest throughout my four years at St. Andrews. Mother drove me to my first class each morning and picked me up wherever my last class was located in the afternoon. By the end of my freshman year, Mother swore that once she cranked the car, it automatically headed for Laurinburg. I felt free and happy: free, because the St. Andrews campus had been designed for wheelchair accessibility; happy, because as a music major, I at last had the opportunity to build on the foundation that Faye Griggs and Fay McLaurin had so painstakingly laid.

I initially worried that the long commute might impinge on Mother's freedom, but she found the best possible way to utilize her time on campus—by playing tennis. She made discreet inquiries and learned that the wife of the dean of admissions played regularly. She and Mother became friends; soon Mother had joined a group of faculty wives for a weekly doubles match. (I raised no objections, since none of them had direct connections to the School of Music.)

When I entered St. Andrews in 1964, the core of its liberal arts curriculum was "Christianity and Culture" (C&C)—a team-taught, multidisciplinary course tracing the history, religion, philosophy, and art of Western civilization. This unique, groundbreaking project must have required tremendous dedication, planning, and organization on the part of the St. Andrews faculty.

None of my high school classes prepared me for C&C's fast-paced, packed-with-content approach. At every turn, C&C took me out of my comfort zone, introducing me to new ideas or requiring me to confront familiar material in unfamiliar ways: I began to comprehend the criteria that separate "good" art from "great" art. I engaged the Bible not only as a religious document, but also from the perspective of scholars who seek to identify its original sources, unravel its chronology, and explain its ambiguities. I compared and contrasted the ideas of history's most prominent philosophers. I became a more discerning, more articulate, more "civilized" person (in the best sense of the word) as a result of my C&C experience—which is, I suspect, the outcome the St. Andrews faculty had in mind when they designed the course.

ALTHOUGH I HAD BEEN EXPERIMENTING WITH CREATIVE WRITING since the age of twelve, I knew that verbal expression was, and always would be, my second love. However, my English professors at St. Andrews made an earnest attempt to rearrange my priorities.

In my freshman English class, the study of Edgar Lee Masters's *Spoon River Anthology* suddenly came to life when the professor, Grace Gibson, gave an extra credit assignment that dealt with death: We were to compose our own series of interrelated poetic epitaphs, using Masters as a general model. I received an "A" for my *Cripple Creek Anthology*.

The following year, I took English Literature as an elective with Professor Margaret Moore, who turned out to be a tennis buff. She had heard of Mother's prowess on the court and requested a lesson; Mother happily obliged. Imagine my shock when Mother reported that Mrs. Moore had been much less interested in tennis than in discussing my future. It seems that Mrs. Moore and Mrs. Gibson had put their heads together and decided that I should pursue a career in English, not music. They thought Mother would join their ranks and persuade me to change my major. Politely but firmly, Mother set the record straight: "Vickie loves music more than anything else in the whole world. I would never even consider asking her to alter her career choice, though I would support any decision she made on her own initiative." I hugged Mother and told her that she had said exactly the right thing.

My feelings of flattery soon gave way to confusion. Why had Mrs. Moore spoken only to Mother, not to me? To what extent had my disability influenced her decision not to approach me directly? I never understood Mrs. Moore's behavior and never mentioned the incident to her. Since I had no intention of changing my major, further discussion seemed pointless.

MY MUSIC CLASSES AT ST. ANDREWS were quite small and 99 percent female. (The latter statistic was a source of disappointment for me.) As I began to get acquainted with the girls, Mother suggested that I invite them to our home for dinner in groups of three or four. They eagerly accepted, welcoming an escape from college cafeteria food. For these festive Friday night gatherings, Daddy provided transportation, while Mother spared no trouble in preparing the meals. She set up the dining room table, used the best china, and planned elaborate menus, complete with multiple dessert choices. Mother later commented wryly that we cleaned our plates so thoroughly, she almost didn't need to wash them.

DR. HERBERT HORN, my piano professor during my freshman and sophomore years, was a brilliant musician and fine teacher. I admired and respected him, but I've always been somewhat puzzled by his conservative approach to my piano playing. I had expected to be assigned difficult, complex, challenging repertoire; instead, Dr. Horn consistently chose music that was actually "easier" than the pieces I had learned with Fay McLaurin in high school. I suspect that my physical limitations may have influenced his attitude. Perhaps Dr. Horn mistook my disability for fragility and feared that I might injure my seemingly vulnerable right hand. Perhaps he thought that technical challenges might impede my artistry at the keyboard. He tried to interest me in composition, but I clearly possessed no talent in this area.

Had I continued to study with Dr. Horn, I might have become a competent, but timid, pianist with modest career ambitions; however, his decision to leave St. Andrews for the North Carolina School of the Arts in Winston-Salem brought about a series of events that dramatically changed the course of my life.

IN THE SPRING of 1966, the St. Andrews campus buzzed with the news that Dady Mehta, first cousin of renowned orchestral conductor Zubin Mehta, would be joining our piano faculty in the fall. Born in Shanghai of Parsi Indian parents, Dady had received his musical training in Paris and Vienna. He and his wife, Martha, had moved to the United States in 1963 so that their son could be born on American soil; they planned to make this country their home. This impressive and exotic background aroused the curiosity of every music student, particularly the piano majors. We were prepared to be star struck—and we were not disappointed.

More than forty years later, I finally heard the story of Dady's curiosity about *me* when the Director of the School of Music told him that one of his best students was in a wheelchair. As a prelude, I must explain that Dady's religion is Zoroastrianism, which places a high premium on honesty. Zoroastrians do not lie. Highly skeptical that anyone with severe physical limitations could successfully pursue a career in piano, Dady had convinced himself that he would have to be the one to tell me I had chosen the wrong field. In this instance, he did not look forward to telling the truth; in fact, he actually dreaded meeting me.

As Dady tells it, at my first lesson he went straight to the window and looked out, not daring to watch me play. "Then suddenly I heard a beautiful sound, a wonderful chord, and more very, very beautiful sounds. I turned around and was not able to comprehend fully how you were playing. With your right hand, you could reach only a seventh, not an octave. You pedaled with the left leg, from the hip! Yet this remarkable achievement was right there in front of my eyes and ears. In the end, I was the one who learned a lot from you!"

Dady has frequently told another story. After I had studied with him for almost a year, he interrupted me in the middle of a piece and shouted, "Vickie!"

I stopped, turned toward him, and asked sheepishly, "Yes, Mr. Mehta, what's the matter?"

He said, "Vickie, you just played your first wrong note!"

He pointed out the error; I made the correction. We both smiled, and the lesson continued. I must confess that this incident is not clear in my memory, but I would never question the veracity of a Zoroastrian.

Dady's approach to teaching proved to be anything but conservative. He assigned the most difficult repertoire I had ever played, then showed me how to "adapt" and "edit" troublesome passages so that I could play them securely and convincingly. Much of the piano literature, previously off-limits, suddenly opened up to me. My burgeoning technique astonished no one more than Fay McLaurin, who had never taught me conservatively.

Dady awakened my pianistic sense of adventure. I became a bold performer, willing to test my limits at the keyboard, constantly striving to play the most challenging repertoire within my capabilities. Thanks to Dady, I had discovered that those capabilities were far broader than I had ever imagined. This is the spirit I took with me to graduate school and into my professional career. I had learned to dream big.

Dady's intense interest in my career was self-evident, but I did not foresee the lengths to which he and Martha would eventually go to help me realize my goals—and I certainly would not have predicted our close, lifelong friendship. In future years, many academic professionals would support and encourage me, but none surpassed the Mehtas in loyalty, devotion, and personal concern.

Two circumstances surrounding my senior recital at St. Andrews on March 29, 1968, are permanently etched in my mind. First, my program, selected by Dady, encompassed an extremely ambitious array of repertoire, ranging from J.S. Bach to a set of unpublished contemporary pieces by Lucia Alcalay, a Viennese composer and personal friend of Dady's. My performance was their United States premiere—a rare opportunity for a twenty-two-year-old undergraduate. Second, I became ill with a virus that gave me a severely upset stomach. I left my bed only for frequent trips to the bathroom. Dady spoke to Mother daily by phone: "Tell Vickie not to practice—she knows the music. Just tell her to rest and recover." Adding to my stress was the imminent arrival of my father's Virginia relatives, including Aunt Victoria, who had never heard me play onstage. I had to pull myself together—the quicker, the better.

By the evening of March 29, I still felt a bit shaky, but the enormity of the occasion—and the large, enthusiastic audience— inspired me to play with gusto and confidence. When I saw the beautiful flowers sent by well-wishers, I told Mother that if, by chance, I expired during the performance, they could proceed with the funeral right away and on the premises. (That must have really calmed her nerves.)

Dady called my playing that night "superb" and said he would be giving me a recital grade of "A." In my opinion, he didn't give me the "A." I earned it!

THE MUSIC THEORY DEPARTMENT at St. Andrews consisted of one woman—my faculty adviser, Dr. Helen Rogers. She taught theory, sixteenth-century and eighteenth-century counterpoint, and musical form. Demanding and relentless in the classroom, she also had a twinkle in her eye. I surmised that her tough exterior concealed a heart of gold. On more than one occasion, she proved me right.

Sometime during my junior year, I decided that I didn't want my B.M. degree to be "terminal," so I approached Helen with a bold plan: I wanted to go to graduate school and prepare myself to teach at the college level. Her only reservation echoed my own thoughts: Could I make such a huge physical adjustment? It was a legitimate concern, since I still lived with my parents and relied on Mother for transportation as well as daily chores like dressing and undressing. In fact, emotionally and physically, I had been in the protective womb of my family my entire life. I had never spent even one night away from them. Was I now ready to enter the real world, cut the umbilical cord, and live independently?

Sensing my resolve and taking a leap of faith, Helen agreed to investigate graduate schools that had outstanding music programs and were physically accessible for wheelchairs. The short list consisted of the University of Illinois, the University of Missouri, and UCLA.

I don't remember exactly when I told my parents about my meeting with Helen, but they received the news calmly and thoughtfully. They could have discouraged me. They could have (with some justification) questioned my sanity. Instead, they remained cool, keeping their doubts to themselves or discussing them with each other privately. They simply told me to go ahead with my plans, saying that we'd see how things went.

Many years later, Martha and Dady told me that Mother had visited them at their home in Laurinburg for a long talk about choosing the right university for me. Of course, they were all focused on wheelchair accessibility and the excellence of the music program, but Mother was particularly concerned with my basic physical and emotional survival in a foreign environment. I believe that the Mehtas' emphatic, enthusiastic "thumbs up" gave Mother the courage she needed to support my plans without reservation. From then on, my dream became her dream.

Helen and I had agreed that I should choose an academic music curriculum in which my disability would not be a factor, so I applied at Illinois, Missouri, and UCLA as a Master of Music degree candidate in Musicology (music history and research).

I had been hoping for some sort of financial aid. The breakthrough came as a result of Dady's having nominated me for a Woodrow Wilson Fellowship. I received an Honorable Mention rating, prompting the University of Illinois to offer me a waiver of tuition and fees for my first year of graduate study. It seemed that my bold plan just might become a reality.

The approach of graduation brought the unexpected news that I was once again class valedictorian, but the satisfaction of this accomplishment paled in comparison with the raw excitement of my preparations for the future.

These three interrelated poetic "epitaphs," part of an English assignment at St. Andrews, were modeled loosely after those of Edgar Lee Masters's "Spoon River Anthology." I called my version "Cripple Creek Anthology."

FLORENCE MOCKINGBIRD

My whole life was spent in doing good deeds!
I tended the sick; I cared for the poor;
I delivered new babies; I buried the dead;
And never one penny did I get.

I saved the life of Jonathan Smith
When he was ill with typhoid fever.
I nursed him day and night for weeks
And marveled at youth's will to live.

Then he grew up—a strong, proud man
Who would not stoop to speak to me.
And as I passed him on the street,
I marveled at man's vanity.

One by one they all grew up—
Strong, proud men and fine young girls
Who would not stoop to speak to me.
Then at the annual town picnic
The noble inhabitants of Cripple Creek
Gave their highest honor, the citizenship badge,
To Roy Slicktongue, the politician!

Never one penny did I get—
Yet I tended the sick; I cared for the poor;
I delivered new babies; I buried the dead . . .
My whole life was wasted in doing good deeds!

JONATHAN SMITH

When I was only eight
I first met Death.
And if it had not been for Florence Mockingbird
The meeting would have been permanent.

She saved my life, and I was grateful to her.
As I grew up, I wanted to thank her.
But every time I passed her on the street
Her hard, cold face, her lifeless stare and bitter smile
Made the words stick in my throat.

I often marveled that she who could give life to others
Did not know how to live herself.

SLICKTONGUE

Twice elected Councilman, three times Mayor,
Four times Senator, and finally—
Citizen of the Year!
The crowning accomplishment
Of a life dedicated in service
To the people of Cripple Creek.
On countless occasions I proclaimed the motto
That brought me success:
"If it's good enough for the people of Cripple Creek,
It's good enough for Roy Slicktongue!"

Actually, I suppose a more accurate version would have been:
"If it's good enough for Roy Slicktongue,
It had better be good enough for the people of Cripple Creek!"

46

SENIOR RECITAL AT ST. ANDREWS COLLEGE

Laurinburg, N.C.
March 29, 1968

Klavierübung III (Four Duets) .... Bach
    E Minor
    F Major
    G Major
    A Minor

Five Little Two-Voice Studies for Piano (1955) .... Lucia Alcalay
    Andante
    Allegro
    Lento
    Improvisando
    Vivace

INTERMISSION

Two Preludes (from Volume One) .... Debussy
    The Girl with the Flaxen Hair
    The Interrupted Serenade

Moment Musical No. 6 .... Schubert
    Allegretto

Sonata in D Major (ca. 1771/1773) .... Haydn
    Allegro
    Adagio
    Tempo di Minuet

CHAPTER FOUR

CHAMPAIGN-BOUND —
BUT NOT WITHOUT MY PANTYHOSE!

THE UNIVERSITY OF ILLINOIS at Urbana-Champaign (UIUC), thanks to the pioneering efforts of Timothy J. Nugent, was the first U.S. campus to be made physically accessible for returning disabled veterans of World War II. Knowing that the university had welcomed these wounded warriors, I assumed the red carpet would be ready and waiting for me. To my surprise and dismay, the Rehabilitation Division informed me that although I had been accepted by the School of Music, I must also be personally interviewed and evaluated by the rehab staff before my admission to the master's program would be official. I could only hope and pray that this unforeseen circumstance would not foil my plans.

Springing into action, Mother made flight reservations to Champaign for the two of us, while I called the musicology and piano department chairmen to set up appointments with them during my time on campus. I explained to the piano chairman, Professor Dean Sanders, that although I would be majoring in musicology, I wanted to continue my piano study as an elective. He said I would have to audition for, and be accepted by, the piano faculty. This trip had assumed momentous significance.

During our jam-packed, three-day visit in April, Mother and I accomplished all our goals. The assistant director of the rehabilitation center, Joseph Konitzki, gave us a guided tour, fielded our questions, and arranged for us to visit Allen Hall, the dorm where I'd probably be living. Mr. Konitzki's calm, reassuring demeanor convinced Mother and me that maybe it really would be okay for me to go to school so far from home.

When I told the physical therapist that my mother dressed and undressed me, he looked horrified, until I quickly added that I was ready, willing, and eager to establish my independence. We analyzed my specific needs and discussed various gadgets that might help me. Daddy had already given me a long shoehorn that worked nicely for putting on my shoes. For back zippers, the therapist suggested a zipper pull with a long extension. Then he showed me a pair of yard-long wooden handles with a smooth, curved surface at the end. These were used to hold underwear and slacks in place so that I could slip my feet and legs into them. There was nothing, however, to help me with pantyhose, only a "sock aid." When the therapist suggested that I could simply wear socks all the time, I refrained from comment, but thought to myself, "Not on your life." There are some things a girl should never have to give up—not even for the sake of independence!

At my piano audition, I announced that I would begin by playing several unpublished two-voice studies by Lucia Alcalay. As I expected, the piano professors asked to see the score of this unfamiliar music and were quite interested to learn that these studies were actually contemporary two-part inventions, with no key or meter signatures. I think the faculty was delighted to hear totally fresh and new pieces of piano repertoire. The remainder of my audition also went well; in a few weeks, I received a letter from Professor Sanders, confirming that I could study piano for elective credits.

The only negative aspect of my meeting with the head of musicology, Dr. Bruno Nettl, came with his disclosure that musicology classes did not meet in Smith Hall (the main music building), but in old houses on nearby Nevada Street. Those buildings had neither ramps nor elevators. Furthermore, an elevator was being installed in Smith with no guarantee that it would be completed by September. UIUC's stellar reputation for accessibility had apparently been grossly exaggerated. I strongly suspected that few (if any) of those WWII vets had been musicologists or pianists.

THE TEAM EFFORT OF "GETTING VICKIE READY FOR ILLINOIS" consumed the entire summer of 1968. In my weekly piano lessons with Dady, I prepared the music I would play at the first lesson with my new teacher. Since the musicology department required a working knowledge of German, Helen Rogers gave me a beginning level German text, so I'd have a head start.

On the home front, Mother took me shopping for clothes, as well as a bedspread and curtains for my dorm room. Every day I meticulously practiced dressing and undressing myself with my various gadgets, but the nagging question of my pantyhose remained. Mother had bought me stylish new outfits, and I had no intention of wearing them with socks. We had been telling our friends to keep their ears open, in case they heard of a device that might solve this problem; but with summer drawing to a close, I began to feel desperate.

One night a dear friend, Betty Watson, called from Ridge Spring, South Carolina, to say that she and her husband Joe had attended a party in Columbia where they had met a physical therapist who had a device specifically for putting on hose. Betty added that they hadn't planned to go to the party, but they had changed their minds at the last minute. We agreed that a Higher Power must have influenced that decision. Of course, we were ecstatic. Joe purchased the device for me the next day and drove to

Bennettsville to deliver it to my doorstep. It proved to be the trickiest of my gadgets, but after a few frustrating attempts, I mastered the strategy.

With the last piece of the puzzle in place, I felt about as ready as I could be for the biggest challenge of my life.

CHAPTER
FIVE

REWRITING MOZART: GRAD SCHOOL, MUSICOLOGY, AND MATURITY

SHORTLY BEFORE LABOR DAY 1968—in the wee hours of the morning, our car packed to the hilt—Mother, Daddy, and I left Bennettsville to make the seventeen-hour drive to Illinois. I tried to sleep in the back seat, but my mind was bursting with anticipation, excitement, and sheer terror.

When we arrived the next morning at Room 66 in Allen Hall, my roommate, Phyllis Goren, was already there. Seeing her in a motorized wheelchair with very little use of her hands, I understood why she had not answered the letter I had sent her during the summer. I had assumed that my roommate would be able-bodied, but here was someone much more disabled than I. We learned that Phyllis had flown in from Denver with no one to help her get settled; so after unpacking and organizing my belongings, Mother and Daddy plunged in and did the same for her.

Phyllis and I were never close friends, but I respected and admired her for pursuing her master's in sociology while coping with a progressive terminal illness. The severity of her physical problems made my disability seem like a mere inconvenience.

Finally, the dreaded moment arrived: my parents' departure for South Carolina, *without me*. We were in the hallway at the rehab center. I had expected Mother to cry, but when I saw that Daddy's eyes were brimming with tears, my carefully guarded composure collapsed. Mother hugged me hard, and Daddy leaned over to kiss my cheek. I wanted to tell them not to worry, that I would be okay, but the words stuck in my throat.

As soon as they were out of sight, I made a beeline for the nearest bathroom and went in one of the stalls, where I sobbed loudly for quite a long time. Fortunately, someone entered the room, forcing me to at least try to pull myself together. "Okay," I thought, "Be calm. Enough histrionics." My mind shifted to Phyllis. I pictured her in her motorized chair. I could hardly imagine the difficulties she faced. Compared to her, I was virtually able-bodied. Suddenly my tears seemed selfish and foolish. I resolved to spend more time helping her, less time worrying about myself.

I knew the coming weeks would bring difficult adjustments. It would be silly to think otherwise. I also knew that my anxieties would not disappear overnight. Perhaps I would spend the entire fall semester "learning the ropes" of my new life. Deep down, however, I believed that I had made a good decision in coming to Illinois. I remained committed to teaching at the college level someday, and I would do whatever it took to prepare for that career. But why, oh why, couldn't the University of South Carolina have been on Helen Rogers's short list?

The physical absence of my family and friends engulfed me in loneliness, but were not these wonderful people with me in spirit? I took comfort in naming them one-by-one: Mother, Daddy, Mary Jo, Helen Rogers, the Mehtas, Fay McLaurin, the Men's Bible Class. Had not they, and many others, expressed their love and support? Surely I could count on that love and support to pull me through those times when I might be tempted to cave in and give up.

I began to feel a bit more peaceful. My fears persisted, but the panic had subsided. I drew a deep breath, closed my eyes, and prayed that God would give me the strength and courage I needed to do my best every single day. The final outcome of this adventure

I would leave in His hands.

After a few minutes, I wiped away my tears, blew my nose, and wheeled myself out into the hallway, determined to greet everyone I met with a smile and a cheery "Hello."

THOSE FIRST FEW WEEKS OF SEPARATION were indeed harrowing for me, but they were probably even worse for Mother. After all, she had protected me and taken care of me *every day* for twenty-two years. She must have feared constantly for my well-being, if not my very survival. About a year later, she told me that Daddy had driven all seventeen hours back to South Carolina because she couldn't stop crying. After about a month, she said, she could at last go out in public and answer questions about "how Vickie is doing" without collapsing into tears.

In my first letter home (September 11, 1968), I tried to be reassuring: "I get periodic waves of homesickness when I think I just can't stand it another minute, but this passes when I think about what a truly wonderful place this is." A month later, though still struggling, I remained optimistic: "I am just doing the best I can each day and trying not to worry beyond that. Even if I don't succeed here, I will always be glad that I came and made the effort. The experiences I've had and the people I've met more than make up for the difficulties. However, I am going on the assumption that I will make it and that things will eventually get a little easier."

The stress and anxiety of these tumultuous life changes caused my monthly female cycle to shut down for almost a year. Mother and I were apprehensive until our family doctor in Bennettsville assured us that once I had adjusted—physically and emotionally— to my new environment, my body would return to normal. He was right, but in the meantime, my roommate, aware of the situation, teased me mercilessly about "keeping such late hours after those concerts." I jokingly replied, "Look, Phyl, the most obvious explanation is the only one I can definitely rule out!"

I gradually became acclimated to the routines of dorm life and began to enjoy the easy, friendly camaraderie with the other residents in the cafeteria and community bathroom. I even learned to operate the washing machines in the laundry room. Because of my youthful appearance and thick drawl, everyone wanted to know: "Are you a freshman?" and "What part of the South are you from?" In retrospect, I think I was noticed more for my accent than my disability.

I soon picked up the unique lingo used by the other physically disabled students. The Rehabilitation-Education Center was simply "The Center." Students with disabilities were "Rehabs," the able-bodied population, "ABs." Rehabs liked to say, "There are always plenty of ABs around, except when you really need one." Rehabs sometimes referred to themselves as "Gimps," but ABs' use of this pejorative term was deemed crude and inappropriate.

I noticed that while ABs tended to be curious about my disability—its cause, how it affected my daily life, etc.—Rehabs seldom discussed these matters. The assumption was that each person dealt with his own problems in his own way. I don't even remember what illness Phyllis had; I don't think she ever told me.

The Center operated a fleet of accessible buses that followed prescribed hourly routes, picking up Rehabs and transporting them to and from classes. We quickly committed to memory all information pertaining to the bus schedules as well as the idiosyncrasies of the bus drivers.

Martin Cox, my favorite bus driver, told us up front: "I may be on time or late, but never early!" Martin knew when each of us had classes, and he'd wait a few extra minutes if we weren't in the dorm lobby at the appointed time. His homespun philosophy brightened our days: "No matter what you want to do," he mused, "it's either illegal, immoral, or causes cancer." Martin introduced me to Baskin-Robbins ice cream and personally recommended pralines 'n cream: No wonder I fell in love with him.

SINCE THERE WERE ONLY ABOUT A DOZEN MASTER'S DEGREE CANDIDATES in musicology, we quickly coalesced into a community despite our diverse backgrounds. My classmates readily fell into the routine of helping me in and out of the old houses on Nevada Street—two people supporting me as I negotiated the four or five steps, a third person lifting my manual wheelchair. From time to time, the professors also participated in this ritual.

My music history classes at St. Andrews had focused on mainstream classical music, but musicology was a whole new ballgame with its emphasis on research and music that seemed far out of the mainstream. For Professor Herbert Kellman's Introduction to Musicology, I had to write a big term paper on "The State of Research in English Music of the Fourteenth and Early Fifteenth Centuries." Although I initially considered the topic to be the height of esotericism, the research proved to be quite fascinating. I received an "A" on the paper; Professor Kellman commented favorably on my content, organization, and the neatness of my typing. I found the latter amusing, since I had hired a professional typist.

Professor Isaac Thomas's lectures in Ancient and Medieval Music were surprisingly accessible, but we had only one big test the entire semester. (I had discovered this to be the rule, not the exception, in graduate level courses.) On December 4, I wrote to Mother and Daddy: "Good news today! I made "A" on my Ancient and Medieval test. When Professor Thomas gave me my paper, he said it was excellent, adding that he'd like to keep it for a while, because if some of the other students come in complaining about their grades, he can show them my paper as an example of how the questions should have been answered."

A required two-semester course called The History of Musical Notation proved to be my biggest headache. Professor Scott Goldthwaite's laid-back joviality did nothing to ameliorate the mind-boggling nature of the subject matter. Week after week, we transcribed ancient manuscripts into modern musical notation, using complicated rules and formulas, which I never understood. The virtually incomprehensible textbook might as well have been written in a foreign language.

When I noticed that Nancy Stagg, who sat across the table from me, had a confused look on her face, I summoned my courage, approached her after class, and asked if she felt as lost in this course as I did. Her affirmative response launched our beautiful friendship. For the remainder of the school year, Nancy and I commiserated over our transcription assignments, occasionally threatening to burn our Notation texts. In June, we heaved sighs of relief, gratefully accepted our "Bs," and moved on.

WHILE MUSICOLOGY TOOK ME INTO UNCHARTED WATERS, my piano study kept me sane and grounded. My new teacher, Thomas Baker, was young, handsome, personable, and (not incidentally) an excellent musician. A graduate of Yale, he had interrupted his doctoral studies at UIUC to accept a piano faculty position. Once again, I had exactly the right teacher at exactly the right time.

Because of the inaccessibility of Tom's studio (on the second floor of an old house on Nevada Street), he arranged for me to have my weekly lessons in a first-floor studio in Smith Hall. Practicing posed a thornier problem: Practice rooms in Smith were on the third floor, and the elevator was not yet usable.

Consequently, for almost three months, I had to practice on two small, out-of-tune, totally inadequate instruments at Allen Hall.

At my first lesson, I played Mozart's *Sonata in A Major, K. 331,* which I had learned with Dady Mehta over the summer. The first movement, in "theme-and- variations" form, contains one variation in which the right hand has nothing but parallel octaves. Since I could reach only a seventh, Dady and I had edited that variation, leaving the melody line the same, but changing the lower notes so that I was playing thirds and sixths. We considered the result to be quite satisfactory.

I gave Tom this explanation before playing the piece. He looked a bit skeptical and probably thought, "She's rewriting Mozart?" At the end of the movement, I turned toward him anxiously. His broad grin spoke volumes; he loved it.

In the following weeks, I polished the Mozart and added new repertoire: three Bach preludes and fugues, another Mozart sonata, four Chopin mazurkas, a Chopin nocturne, and Ernest Bloch's *Poems of the Sea* (a set of three "atmospheric" pieces). With the completion of the long-awaited elevator in mid-November, I could finally dig in and practice productively. I wrote to Mother and Daddy on November 19: "Yesterday I practiced in Smith from noon to 3:30 p.m. nonstop! It was so great to be in a practice room, I just couldn't quit."

Although I was studying piano as an elective, Tom obviously regarded me as a serious piano student— a performance major. I was in heaven.

I had been attending the piano department's student recitals on Tuesday mornings in Smith Recital Hall. When Tom suggested that I play the Mozart *A Major Sonata* on one of these programs, I jumped at the chance.

My University of Illinois performing debut on March 18, 1969, proved that I could hold my own with the university's piano majors. Student and faculty comments were entirely favorable. Since no one raised the slightest objection to the edited variation, I concluded that if Mozart had had my right hand, he would have written it my way to start with!

Nancy Stagg gave me a long-stemmed red rose in honor of the occasion. Phyllis also attended, parking her motorized chair at the front of the hall so that I could see her smiling face as I wheeled onto the stage. Unable to applaud with her hands, she called out a resounding "Bravo!" as I took my final bow.

I NEVER REGRETTED my year as Phyllis's roommate, but I longed for my own space. Only the resident advisors in Allen Hall had private rooms and private baths, so with a strong ulterior motive, I asked the advisor on my floor for information about the job. The benefits astounded me—free tuition, free room-and-board, plus a small monthly salary. The responsibilities included administrative duties (working in the dorm office and supervising room assignments each semester) and general counseling as needed. The position required no special training—just empathy and a little organization. So far, so good.

When I met with Allen Hall's head resident, whom I knew fairly well, she urged me to apply for an advisorship and offered to write a recommendation for me. For once in my life, my physical disability proved to be an advantage. In the late 1960s, the university was striving to make its residence hall staffs "representative" of the student body. Being in a wheelchair made me the logical choice to represent the sizable Rehab population of Allen Hall.

During my four years as a residence hall advisor, I learned that the most demanding aspect of the job was its unpredictability. I had to be ready at a moment's notice to do whatever it took to keep dorm life running smoothly—not an easy assignment for someone like me, who preferred a structured, orderly schedule.

One day a couple of the girls on my floor rushed up to me: "Vickie! Some boys [from a nearby dorm] are raiding our ice machine! They're loading ALL the ice into large bags!"

"Quick!" I said. "Push me to the vending room as fast as you can!" We went speeding down the hall.

Confronting the culprits—obviously caught red-handed—I demanded, "What do you think you're doing? This ice is for Allen Hall residents and you are *not* Allen Hall residents!"

They immediately backed down and began to apologize: "We're sorry, but the ice machine in our dorm is broken."

"That doesn't matter!" I insisted. "You have no right to take our ice without asking permission."

"Do you want us to put it back?" they asked contritely.

"You may keep a small amount," I said, "but yes, I want you to put the rest of it back." They dutifully obeyed.

News of this narrowly averted crisis soon spread throughout the dorm. When the head resident praised me for having "stood up" to the intruders, I explained, gently and tactfully, that I had managed the entire rescue operation while sitting in my wheelchair.

I WAS STILL BASKING in the glow of my triumph as a resident advisor when Tom made a startling remark at one of my lessons: "The repertoire you've learned would make a great recital program. Would you be interested in playing a solo recital next year?"

I contained my euphoria long enough to say, "Wait—I'm a musicology major, studying piano as an elective. Would I be allowed to present an *elective* recital?"

"Why not?" Tom responded. He then added that he would make an official request with Dean Sanders, the piano department chairman, and that I would probably have to play a longer-than-usual "jury" (piano parlance for "final exam") at the end of the semester. The faculty would evaluate my performance and render its verdict. The jury went well; I *could* play a solo recital during the 1969-70 academic year. The only stipulation was that I not play in the spring, when the calendar would be crowded with required recitals. I went to the School of Music office, signed up for November 21, and scurried off to my practice room.

MY SEARCH FOR A MASTER'S THESIS TOPIC was an exercise in futility until Nancy Stagg recommended that I consult one of UIUC's most distinguished musicologists, Dr. Alexander Ringer. I knew Dr. Ringer only by reputation, but Nancy had studied music history with him during her undergraduate years at the University of Oklahoma.

When Dr. Ringer learned that I had majored in piano as an undergraduate, he asked if I'd be interested in a Chopin-related topic. It sounded like a splendid idea. "Are you aware," he continued, "of Chopin's passionate devotion to Italian opera? As a matter of fact, his music is permeated with operatic elements." I had never heard this, and I thought I knew a little something about Chopin. Dr. Ringer also pointed to the scarcity of scholarly research on Chopin's indebtedness to opera, adding that this could be my chance to make a significant contribution to both pianists and musicologists. I knew then that I had found my thesis topic—and my thesis adviser.

We agreed that I would begin work on "Operatic Elements in the Music of Frederic Chopin" the following fall.

REMEMBERING THE ILLNESS that had almost derailed my senior recital at St. Andrews, I dared to hope that I could approach my Illinois performance calmly and without incident. No such luck. On Friday, November 21, 1969, approximately six hours before show time, the unpredictability of my resident advisor's job reared its ugly head.

One of the girls on my floor approached me breathlessly, saying that two of the freshmen girls were fighting.

"You mean actually exchanging blows?" I wanted to get the facts straight.

"Yes," she said.

These girls had never been compatible, but this was big trouble, even for them. I talked with each girl individually, then sat them down together. They promised to refrain from further violence, and I promised they would have different roommates next semester. "Please," I said, "try to hang on and keep the peace."

Having diffused the crisis as best I could, I had to put this squabble out of my mind and concentrate only on Bach, Mozart, Chopin, and Bloch.

My powers of concentration prevailed. The stunningly successful recital effectively established me as a legitimate performing pianist at the University of Illinois, a crucial milestone in my preparation for a college teaching career.

From a personal point of view, I felt extremely gratified that many special people were in the audience: my parents, my dear friend Nancy and other musicology classmates, my former roommate Phyllis, students and staff from Allen Hall, Dean Sanders and other piano professors, Mr. Konitzki and several staff members from the rehab center, and my thesis adviser, Dr. Ringer.

From a pianistic point of view, the recital tapes revealed what I already knew—the performance had not been flawless; however, despite the glitches and wrong notes, my playing sounded authoritative, artistic, and surprisingly mature. The latter I attributed at least in part to my newfound independence. Living on my own seemed to have sharpened my aesthetic sensibilities.

The small-town girl who could barely dress herself when she left rural South Carolina had come a long, long way.

At the post-recital reception, hosted by Tom and his wife at their apartment, the Allen Hall staff presented me with a beautiful music box in the shape of a miniature grand piano. Nancy captured the moment in one of my all-time favorite photographs. Thus began my collection of "little pianos," which now numbers more than thirty.

November 21, 1969: at the post-recital reception in Tom Baker's apartment. Left to right: me, Tom Baker, Mother, and Rigney Cofield, a musicology classmate.

As the evening drew to a close, I tried in vain to find adequate words to thank Tom, whose confidence in me had never wavered and whose initiative had made this wonderful opportunity possible. But when I saw the look of pleasure and pride on his face, I knew that words were unnecessary. Riding back to South Carolina to celebrate Thanksgiving, Mother, Daddy, and I all shed a few tears, but this time they were tears of joy and gratitude.

MY SECOND YEAR OF GRADUATE SCHOOL brought a significant social milestone—my first date! To be precise, a double date. My escort, Randy, and I were in wheelchairs; the others used crutches. We piled into a cab, the driver stashed the chairs in the trunk, and off we went to see *Love Story*. As the tragic plot unfolded, we sat there, crying into our popcorn and having a marvelous time. Arriving back at the dorm, I couldn't help thinking that at the ripe old age of twenty-four, I definitely qualified as a late bloomer, though I quickly reassured myself that it was better to bloom late than not at all.

My subsequent dates, both Rehabs and ABs, were merely lighthearted diversions. Tom Baker, the only man who really "interested" me, provided my most memorable outings, but he was married. His wife spent long periods in Russia researching her dissertation, but I would never have taken advantage of that circumstance to pursue a romantic relationship with him. The very fact that I was tempted made me feel quite mature.

Using the wisdom of hindsight, I now think that I avoided serious personal entanglements primarily because I was single-mindedly focused on my career. As long as my career path remained uncertain, I had to be ready to follow that path wherever it might lead. Being free and unattached meant that I could make those decisions solely for myself.

IN THE SPRING of 1970, I became a licensed Illinois driver, thus qualifying the driver's education instructor at the rehab center as a candidate for sainthood. At the keyboard, I was coordinated and facile; behind the wheel, I was awkward and terrified. My driving lessons assumed a sense of urgency because I had been hired to teach piano at the St. Andrews Summer Music

Camp—my first summer job! I had every intention of being in charge of my own transportation.

The written test posed no problem; I had always been good at comprehending and regurgitating facts. The driving test went well until the officer asked me to make a left turn. As I started to make the turn, the sudden "grab" of the emergency brake on the passenger side of the car told me I'd made a mistake—I wasn't in the left turn lane! I had to endure four more weeks of lessons before I could retake the driving test, which I somehow passed.

BEAUTIFUL, IDYLLIC ALLERTON PARK at Monticello, Illinois, provided the perfect setting for a piano teachers conference at the end of April. Having survived the rigors of driver's education, I looked forward to enjoying the natural wonders of the park as well as the musical stimulation of the conference.

I played Haydn's *Variations in F Minor* in a recital of advanced piano students at Allerton House, a lovely old mansion with a library that had been converted into a small concert hall. I don't recall the circumstances of my selection for this performance, but I considered it a great honor to be the only musicology major on the program.

The conference concluded the following day. As I approached the bus that would take students back to the university, Tom asked me if I'd like to join him for some sightseeing at Allerton. I quickly told the bus driver I didn't need a ride. For the next four hours, Tom and I had a ball, as he later said, "going places no self-respecting wheelchair should go!" Leaving behind the public trails, we explored areas of the park seldom seen by tourists.

As we made our way back to Champaign, we realized that Allen Hall's cafeteria would be closed by the time we arrived, so Tom and I stopped at an Italian restaurant for the best lasagna I've ever tasted. Driving through Campus Town, we noticed that the local theater was featuring Walt Disney's *Fantasia*, which neither of us had ever seen. We were just in time for the show.

Since 1970, I have spent every May first reliving, at least for a few moments, the happiness and exhilaration of that magical day.

WHEN I ARRIVED IN BENNETTSVILLE for the summer, I had my Illinois license transferred to South Carolina, and I began to solidify my driving skills by going to and from St.Andrews in my parents' old Studebaker. Traversing the same route Mother and I had taken hundreds, if not thousands, of times, I relished my new status as a faculty member at the college where I had recently been a student and wondered if maybe, just maybe, I would someday have a full-time job.

OF THE MANY COMPLIMENTS I received after my 1969 recital, Dr. Ringer's had been the most extravagant: "Your playing is marvelous. You are a true musician." Turning to Nancy, he added, "She could teach the teachers around here a thing or two." That comment notwithstanding, in September 1970, he reminded me, gently but firmly, that musicology, not piano, should be my top priority and that the time had come to finish the thesis. I knew better than to argue. There would be no recital that year.

Well in advance of my twenty-fifth birthday on February 11, 1971, the girls on my floor (most of them freshmen) began teasing me: "You'll be a quarter of a century old!" They emphasized the word *old*.

As I left my room that morning, I had a slight premonition of impending mischief. Upon my return, I saw a few strips of toilet paper draped across the outside of my door with a birthday card attached. Girls began streaming out of their rooms singing, "Happy Birthday to you" . . . " I unlocked my door and found myself confronted with the most thorough, massive, and artistic T.P. job

I've ever seen.

The ring leaders of the plot explained that the head resident had given them the master key so they could carry out their plans and that she awaited us in her apartment with cake and punch. We had a delightful party, after which I said jokingly, "Look, in case you haven't noticed, I'm in a wheelchair, so I expect you to clean up the mess in my room!" They happily complied, or so it seemed. That night, as I pulled back my bedspread, I discovered my pillow tightly and neatly wrapped in toilet paper. Too bad it was dormitory standard versus a brand known for its softness.

AS TRIPS TO DR. RINGER'S OFFICE BECAME MORE FREQUENT, he became quite adept at hoisting my chair and me up the steps. In fact, if Dr. Nettl happened to be passing by and offered assistance, Dr. Ringer would brush him aside: "Out of the way, Bruno! I don't need any help, but if you insist on being useful, how about holding the door?" I struggled to keep a straight face during these exchanges.

Looking back, I realize that the writing of my thesis went relatively smoothly. Most of the revisions Dr. Ringer recommended were minor. Some chapters he accepted verbatim. However, even with a skilled adviser's supervision and guidance, thesis preparation is intense, demanding, physically draining, and emotionally exhausting. I put a sign on my door that read: "Enter with caution. Occupant suffering from thesis trauma!" At the bottom were the words *Write on*, my variation of "Right on," which was just becoming a popular expression of the day.

I submitted "Operatic Elements in the Music of Frederic Chopin," the final requirement for my Master of Music degree in musicology, to the graduate music office on May 14, 1971.

ALTHOUGH THE COMPLETION OF MY MASTER'S provided relief and closure, other developments brought stress, doubt, and uncertainty. Tom had accepted a piano position at Murray State University in Kentucky and would be moving there over the summer. As a teacher and as a friend, he had become an integral part of my life; I could hardly imagine being without him.

I made my final appearance as his student on May 20 in a piano department recital. We played the first two movements of Mozart's *Concerto in A Major, K. 488.*

I have always felt a deep affinity for that piece because of the special circumstances of the occasion and because it is the only concerto I ever performed.

In September 1970, I had registered at the university's Educational Placement Office. My resumé and credentials were sent to numerous schools advertising vacancies for teachers of piano and/or music history. I had precisely one interview—at Hiram College in Hiram, Ohio—and I didn't get the position. Were prospective employers discriminating against me because of my physical disability? Perhaps, but I noticed that my able-bodied classmates weren't being hired either.

What should I do next? Continuing my graduate studies seemed the most logical choice, since I had the security of my residence hall assistantship—but what degree program would be best for me? I politely refused Dr. Ringer's offer to recommend me as a doctoral candidate in musicology (one degree in musicology being quite enough).

Tom suggested a second master's with a major in piano, which, after all, had always been my first love. However, when he made this proposal to the piano faculty, objections were raised. No one questioned my musicianship or dedication; they simply felt that a master's candidate in piano should be physically capable of performing most, if not all, of the standard piano repertoire. Tom's argument—that most able-bodied pianists usually end up as specialists through inclination rather than necessity—did not sway the skeptics. With this door closed, I could only hope that somewhere, somehow, a window would open.

That window did open, thanks to Dr. Ringer's perseverance. He called me one afternoon to tell me that Dr. Charles Leonhard, the music education chairman, had agreed to accept me into the Doctor of Education degree program. Having memorized the university's handbook on doctoral degrees in music, I knew that the Ed.D. in music education had two prerequisites: a master's in music education (or its equivalent) and public school teaching experience. I met neither of these criteria.

I never knew what transpired between Dr. Ringer and Dr. Leonhard. All I know is that Dr. Leonhard waived the pre-requisites, requiring that I take only a few master's level education courses, which seemed perfectly reasonable. I could continue to study piano as an elective. The Ed.D., although not the degree program I would have chosen for myself, seemed to be the most viable option at the time, and pursuing a doctorate would definitely look better on my resume than a second master's. So a deal was struck.

There remained the not-so-small matter of finding a piano teacher. I decided to ask Dean Sanders for several reasons. First, he had been extremely complimentary of my 1969 recital, and I felt we would work well together. Second, in his performances he had impressed me with his musicality and the scope of his repertoire. Finally, when the decision had been made that I would not be allowed to pursue a master's in piano, he had been out of town on sabbatical leave, making him in a sense "above the fray." Before I left Champaign for the summer, I reached him by phone. He readily agreed that I could study with him in the fall.

On my flight to South Carolina for summer vacation, I had much to ponder: a new degree program, a new major, and a new piano professor. Most importantly, I had bought myself more time to look for that ever-elusive job.

UNIVERSITY OF ILLINOIS RECITAL

Smith Music Hall
Urbana, Illinois
November 21, 1969

Preludes and Fugues from "Well-Tempered Clavier," Bk. 1 ... Bach
    B-flat Major
    D Minor
    E Major

Sonata in B-flat Major, K. 570 .... Mozart
    Allegro
    Adagio
    Allegretto

INTERMISSION

Three Mazurkas .... Chopin
    G Major, Op. 50, No. 1
    A Minor, Op. 67, No. 4
    G Minor, Op. 24, No. 1

Nocturne in C-sharp Minor, Op. 27, No. 1 .... Chopin

Poems of the Sea .... Bloch
    Waves
    Chanty
    At Sea

FINDING MY NICHE IN
MUSIC EDUCATION

WHEN I MET DR. CHARLIE LEONHARD in 1971, I immediately saw that he exuded the confidence and authority befitting an iconic music educator and author. As chairman of the entire music education curriculum at UIUC, he wielded absolute power. I had heard that having him on your side was tantamount to having God on your side.

With his bald head, rotund physique, and ubiquitous cigarette, he looked like no other professor I had ever seen. His lectures, sprinkled with four-letter words and outrageous anecdotes, sounded like no other lectures I had ever heard. He absolutely mesmerized me.

Dr. Leonhard and I got along famously from the start. I found him to be charming, caring, unfailingly candid, and willing more than once to use his considerable clout on my behalf.

Having entered music education at the doctoral level, with no preamble or preparation, I felt at times like a fish-out-of-water; however, I discovered my niche when Dr. Leonhard advised me to take courses with Dr. James Lyke, UIUC's Group Piano Chairman.

Group teaching was the preferred venue for non-piano music majors, whose keyboard requirements included functional skills, such as sight-reading, improvisation, harmonization, and transposition. Classes for beginners generally met in an electronic "piano lab." More advanced classes met in rooms with multiple acoustic (standard) pianos.

I had at least one course in group piano each semester, thus gaining valuable hands-on experience teaching and being taught in group settings. I also became familiar with a variety of excellent pedagogical materials, especially Dr. Lyke's text, *Keyboard Musicianship*. This experience and knowledge proved to be the key that unlocked my professional future.

DEAN SANDERS not only lived up to my expectations as a teacher, but also took a deep personal interest in my career and eventually became a dear friend. Studying with the department head definitely had its advantages; I could simply sign up for a recital date, no official request or special jury required. Studying piano as an elective also had its advantages; I could perform without the pressure of a degree hanging in the balance.

Dean said he had never encountered anyone who liked to be onstage as much as I did—and in 1972, I spent a lot of time onstage, playing three full length recitals in three different locations—Illinois, South Carolina, and Kentucky.

My second solo recital at UIUC on March 13 featured a broad range of repertoire: J.S. Bach's *French Suite in G Major* (a set of seven stylized dances), Ernst Krenek's *Eight Piano Pieces* (1946), a group of Schubert waltzes, several pieces by Chopin, and—for my big, flashy ending—Khachaturian's *Toccata*.

The Bach was note-perfect until four measures from the end of the gigue (final dance) when a momentary lapse in concentration triggered a memory slip. "Didn't you know," Dean told me later, "that the most treacherous part of a piece is *just before* the end, when you tend to let your guard down?" Needless to say, future memory slips were never four measures from the end.

Overall, the recital went well. Even the "blip" in the Bach didn't sound too bad when I heard the tape. Tom Baker's presence in the audience made the occasion truly special. He had driven from Murray, Kentucky, to be there and seemed genuinely pleased with my playing. When he asked if I'd come to Murray State for a guest recital later in the year, I happily agreed. He brought me a beautiful corsage of yellow roses with a card bearing the printed message: "Wishing You A Speedy Recovery," to which he added, "after your taxing performance! With love from Tom."

On June 11, I played the same repertoire in Bennettsville, my first hometown performance since my high school senior recital. The auditorium was filled to capacity, and I received my first standing ovation. A financial grant from the South Carolina Arts Commission had made the event possible: "The S.C. Arts Commission recognizes the number and quality of South Carolina schools and departments of music which yearly graduate exemplary students in vocal and instrumental music. In an effort to encourage these young musicians and those who are studying out-of-state to practice their art in their home communities, the Prophet Grant Award Program was created." The Marlboro Area Arts Council announced that they were the first in our state to receive this award for my concert.

I thoroughly enjoyed being a guest artist at Murray State University on October 29. In addition to Krenek, Schubert, and Khachaturian, the program included two resurrections from the past: the Haydn *F Minor Variations* and Chopin's *Nocturne, Op. 27, No. 1*. While learning new repertoire always excited me, I had begun to understand the benefits and satisfactions of reworking tried-and-true favorites. The Chopin would eventually become my signature piece. I had to go through numerous performances before I felt that I could effectively communicate its emotional depth and exquisite beauty.

DURING MY LAST year as dorm advisor (1972-73), the girls on my floor decided to organize themselves into an Indian tribe, every girl being given an Indian name suited to her personality and/or interests. A paper teepee bearing the name was displayed on each door. They conferred on me the title of "Chief Advisor" and the obviously appropriate name of "Little Rolling Turtle." That appellation has since been incorporated into my e-mail address.

MOTHER AND DADDY drove to Champaign for my UIUC recital on April 5, 1973, and took me back to South Carolina for spring break the next day. However, the whole occasion almost turned into a disaster.

A few weeks earlier, I had contracted a terrible cold, but by April 5 the symptoms had subsided. I thought I had fully recovered. Wrong! About fifteen minutes before performance time, I made the mistake of blowing my nose. Blood gushed from my left nostril! My friend, Anne Turnbaugh, an undergraduate piano major who was with me in the ladies room, rushed to get paper towels while I lay on the couch. Then she went to find Dean Sanders and inform him of the crisis. Soon the blood flow had slowed to a trickle. Dean paced the hallway outside the ladies room, looking (according to Anne) "like an expectant father," and no doubt feeling just as helpless.

I finally began playing at approximately 8:20 p.m. No one in the audience (including my parents) had any idea why the start of the recital had been delayed. The first half of the program consisted of all-new repertoire: Beethoven's *Eleven Bagatelles, Op. 119*, two Brahms intermezzi, and a Liszt waltz. In the second half, I reprised pieces by Schubert, Chopin, and Bloch. The tape of the recital betrayed surprisingly little of the turmoil I felt; I was, in fact, a basket case the entire time, fearing the nosebleed would recur at any moment. Usually I enjoyed performing, but not that night.

MOTHER BEGAN accumulating tennis accolades as soon as I settled into graduate school. Playing in state and national tournaments rekindled her love of the game and her fierce competitive spirit. Between 1972 and 1993, she held twenty-four number-one rankings in her age division (including singles and doubles). Because there were few tournaments at that time for "older" players, Mother generally faced opponents who were ten or fifteen years her junior. For example, in 1972, when she achieved her first South Carolina ranking by placing third in the 35-and-over ladies doubles, she was 53.

IN THE FALL of 1973, leaving dorm life behind, I moved into an efficiency apartment on campus. I enjoyed the independence and the domesticity, but, after four years of noisy commotion at the dorm, what I most appreciated was the *quiet*. In a letter dated September 17, I thanked Mother and Daddy for sending me some extra money. "With rent being almost $100 a month, I will need the extra amount . . . My grocery bill has been averaging about five dollars each week." I had paid a whopping eight cents for the stamp on the envelope.

MY JOB SEARCH brought only an unending series of disappointments. The music consultant at the Educational Placement Office, John Cooksey, had generously waived the fee I should have been paying to have my credentials sent to more than ten schools. "I'll send your credentials *wherever* you want, *whenever* you want, *at no charge*," he assured me. The combined influence of Tom Baker, Dean Sanders, Jim Lyke, Charlie

Leonhard, and Dady Mehta failed to yield even an interview, although from time to time one of them would receive a phone call with the tantalizing information that I was among the "top ten" or "top five" candidates for a position. Being a runner-up got me nowhere; I lost track of exactly how many jobs I applied for.

Convinced that prospective employers were discriminating against me because of my physical disability, Martha Mehta wrote "A Job For Emily," an article based on my background and experience, which was published in the June/July 1973 issue of *The American Music Teacher*. After detailing Emily's (my) credentials, she demanded, "Why does this record simply vanish when a wheelchair is added to the equation?" Her closing argument made the case clearly and eloquently:

Imagine you are an eminent scholar, a campus leader, a person of consequence on your campus. Look down at your legs and ask yourself this question: "Would I have this authority, would I have achieved this status, in a wheelchair?"

Undoubtedly, you would be the same person. But would the same doors have opened? Emily's application, or that of another wheelchair scholar, may be on your desk right now.

MY LAST RECITAL as Dean's student, on April 8, 1974, was one of my most successful programs. The first half offered an effective contrast between the contemporary brilliance of Kabalevsky's *Variations in D Major, Op. 40* and the elegant classicism of Mozart's Variations on *'Unser dummer Pöbel meint', K.455*. After intermission, I played two Chopin etudes, Chopin's *C Minor Polonaise, Op. 40, No. 2*, and Ravel's three-movement *Sonatine*. I enjoyed reworking the Ravel, which I had first learned with Dady at St. Andrews. The highlight of the evening turned out to be the polonaise. I had feared that my technique would not be adequate for its bold opening melody (in left hand octaves), but when I heard the tape, the strength and conviction of my playing amazed me.

HAVING FINISHED my doctoral coursework in the spring of 1974, I debated whether or not to tackle the next hurdle: a two-part written qualifying examination dealing with research methods and current issues in music education. The graduate school grind had left me burnt-out and unmotivated, but I took the exam anyway, passing only the research portion.

I had reached my lowest ebb. With no job—and no prospects—continuing the doctorate seemed futile. I considered setting myself up as an independent piano teacher in Florence, South Carolina, a relatively large city about an hour's drive from Bennettsville. I even called one of Mother's friends who lived in Florence to see what specific neighborhoods she would recommend.

I have never believed in "dumb luck," preferring instead the pragmatic definition that *luck is the point where preparation and opportunity meet.* One afternoon in late May, just such a lucky moment occurred when Jim Lyke called with the news that a member of the UIUC group piano faculty had unexpectedly resigned. Instead of immediately launching a search for a permanent replacement, Jim had decided to create two half-time positions for the 1974-75 school year; he was offering me one of those positions!

Jim said more or less apologetically that my salary would be only $4,000, but I couldn't have cared less about the money. This would be my first opportunity for legitimate teaching experience at a major university. I had grown quite accustomed to living frugally in my efficiency apartment; my happiness had absolutely nothing to do with money.

UNIVERSITY OF ILLINOIS RECITAL
Smith Music Hall

Urbana, Illinois
March 13, 1972

French Suite in G Major...Bach
    Allemande
    Courante
    Sarabande
    Gavotte
    Bourree
    Loure
    Gigue

Eight Piano Pieces (1946) ....Krenek
    1. Etude   5. Nocturne
    2. Invention   6. Waltz
    3. Scherzo   7. Air
    4. Toccata   8. Rondo

INTERMISSION

8 Valses Sentimentales and Walzer .... Schubert

Nocturne in B Major, Op. 32, No. 1 .... Chopin

Four Preludes, Op. 28 ....Chopin
E Major
F-sharp Major
F Major
D-flat Major

Toccata .... Khachaturian

Note: I played this program in Bennettsville, S.C., under the auspices of the Marlboro Arts Council on June 11, 1972.

GUEST RECITAL

Murray State University
Murray, Kentucky
October 29, 1972

Variations in F Minor (Hob. XVII: 6) .... Haydn

Eight Piano Pieces (1946) .... Krenek
    1. Etude   5. Nocturne
    2. Invention   6. Waltz
    3. Scherzo   7. Air
    4. Toccata   8. Rondo

INTERMISSION

Ten German Dances from Op. 33 .... Schubert

Mazurka in A Minor, Op. 17, No. 4 .... Chopin

Nocturne in C-sharp Minor, Op. 27, No. 1 .... Chopin

Toccata .... Khachaturian

UNIVERSITY OF ILLINOIS RECITAL

Smith Music Hall
Urbana, Illinois
April 5, 1973

Eleven Bagatelles, Op. 119 ....Beethoven

Two Intermezzi ....Brahms
    B Minor, Op. 119, No. 1
    B-flat Major, Op. 76, No. 4

Valse oubliée .... Liszt

INTERMISSION

Ten German Dances, Op. 33 .... Schubert

Mazurka in A Minor, Op. 17, No. 4 ....Chopin

Nocturne in C-sharp Minor, Op. 27, No. 1 ....Chopin

At Sea (from "Poems of the Sea") .... Bloch

UNIVERSITY OF ILLINOIS RECITAL

Smith Music Hall
Urbana, Illinois
April 8, 1974

Variations in D Major, Op. 40 .... Kabalevsky

Ten Variations on "Unser dummer Pöbel meint"
(from Gluck's *Pilger von Mekka*), K. 455 .... Mozart

INTERMISSION

Two Etudes (from "Trois Nouvelles Etudes") .... Chopin
A-flat Major
F Minor

Polonaise in C Minor, Op. 40, No. 2 .... Chopin

Sonatine .... Ravel
Modéré
Mouvement de menuet
Animé

CHAPTER
SEVEN

A YEAR OF TEACHING,
A YEAR OF UNCERTAINTY

UPON LEARNING of Jim Lyke's offer, Dr. Leonhard agreed to let me drop out of the doctoral program for at least a year: "If the degree ever becomes important to you, you'll finish it, and if it doesn't, why bother?" His logic made perfect sense. He did point out that the "only" remaining requirements were the qualifying exam and the dissertation, but I hastened to remind him that I had recently failed the major portion of the exam. Moreover, I had no ready ideas for a dissertation topic. In my mind, the "only" mountain left to climb was Everest.

My year of teaching at the University of Illinois proved to be one of those pivotal experiences that validate the past and foreshadow the future. My four sections of piano classes ranged from freshmen beginners (electronic piano lab) to advanced levels (acoustic pianos). As department chairman, Jim Lyke provided a syllabus listing specific proficiencies and skills for each level. His *Keyboard Musicianship* text was supplemented with other recommended materials. For a relative newcomer like me, the atmosphere provided an ideal balance of autonomy and supervision.

MY FACULTY STATUS (albeit only a half-time, one-year appointment) meant that I could play a recital in the Great Hall of the Krannert Center for the Performing Arts. How could I let an opportunity like that pass me by?

I began planning the program over the summer and in September signed up for a date: February 20, 1975. I decided to open with Lucia Alcalay's *Five Two-Voice Studies*, the unpublished pieces I had premiered on my senior recital at St. Andrews. Mastering and memorizing them had been a real feat, and I knew that their brilliant, contemporary style would appeal to a cosmopolitan university audience. For maximum contrast, I concluded the first half with Haydn's sunny, harmonically predictable *Sonata in F Major (No. 38)*.

The all-Chopin second half consisted of four mazurkas, the C-sharp minor *Polonaise, Op. 26, No. 1*, and the *Nocturne in C minor, Op. 48, No. 1*. Both the *Polonaise* and the *Nocturne* were new to me and required skillful adaptation and editing to compensate for my small right hand and narrow reach. Fearful that the *Nocturne* might be too big a piece for my technique, I asked Dean Sanders if I could play it for him. He graciously agreed to listen to the whole program and gave me his unqualified seal of approval.

In January, I began scheduling practice time on the nine-foot Steinway grand piano in the Great Hall. Being onstage, with the massive empty space all around me, I felt totally awe-struck. I could sense the spirits of the musical giants who had performed there. Violinist Isaac Stern had thrilled me with his virtuosity, André Watts had dazzled me with his pianistic wizardry, and numerous faculty recitals had inspired my own dreams of professional success. Now Vickie Covington from Bennettsville, South Carolina, would take that same stage: My performance had to be top-notch.

My apartment was conveniently located diagonally across the

street from the Krannert Center. Given favorable weather, I could "push" the short distance in my manual chair. The day came when I had to cancel a practice session because of a heavy snowfall. Upon learning the reason for my cancellation, Mr. Nash, Krannert's director of maintenance, called to say that he and a couple of his men would *come get me* and personally escort me across the street. The two men used shovels to clear snow from the sidewalk while Mr. Nash pushed me in my chair. I offered to pay them for their services, but they would accept only my heartfelt thanks.

In the weeks leading up to the recital, I struggled to eat and sleep, becoming more tired each day. Knowing that I would need every ounce of my strength for the *Nocturne*, I went to a doctor, who prescribed a small nightly dose of Valium. "This will solve your problems," he predicted, "but there will be *no* refills." I soon realized how easily one might become dependent on these "magic pills."

I played well on February 20. When I listened to the tape, the *Nocturne* sounded quite creditable, although I could tell that on the last page, my technique was stretched to its limits. I never had the guts to play the piece again; the thought of giving this gorgeous, profound work a substandard performance violated all my musical scruples. Having played it successfully once, I was satisfied.

In the audience that night were Mother and Daddy (Miraculously, there was no snow to impede their drive from South Carolina), a host of friends, several former professors, and virtually the entire staff of the rehab center, including my favorite bus driver, Martin. I loved getting the Krannert "star treatment" and carefully saved the sign from my dressing room door: "Reserved for Victoria Covington." Of the many beautiful flowers I received, six long-stemmed red roses from the six students of my advanced piano class especially touched me.

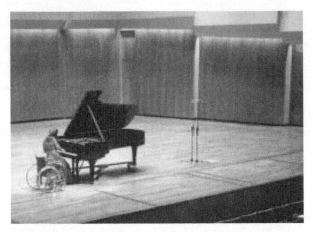

This photo was taken from the balcony during my performance in the Great Hall at the Krannert Center.

THERE WERE TWO JOB INTERVIEWS in early spring 1975—San Francisco State University and California State University at Fullerton. I almost got the position at Fullerton, coming in second to a woman whose husband was a cellist—and the school desperately needed a cellist. (This information came from John Cooksey, the newly hired choral director at Fullerton.)

After completing the interviews, I had a delightful visit in Menlo Park (near San Francisco) with my Great-Aunt Lucy Smith, her daughter Pat, and Pat's husband. I loved hearing Aunt Lucy's reminiscences about the war years when Daddy and Mother were in California and Mother became pregnant with me. Pat and I bonded instantly and still correspond regularly, sharing our love of music as well as other common interests.

I subsequently had a very promising interview at Olivet College in Olivet, Michigan. Everyone I met impressed me favorably. As we toured the nearly finished new music building, they pointed out a spacious room with a gorgeous view that would be my studio, should I be chosen for the job.

On June 13, 1975, the mailman delivered a dozen rejection

letters, each saying, in effect, "Thank you for your application, but the position has been filled." When Mother called, offering to read a letter from Olivet that had been sent to me in Bennettsville, my instincts told me that it would be my thirteenth rejection on that thirteenth day of June. (It was.) Frustration and despair kept me from appreciating the dark humor of the situation. I had expended huge amounts of time and energy applying for jobs. Was all that work for nothing? Would my dream ever be realized?

Sometime that spring, I learned of a vacancy at Baldwin-Wallace College in Berea, Ohio (now Baldwin Wallace University with no hyphen). I looked up Berea on my atlas, noted its location in Northern Ohio next to Lake Erie, and shuddered to think what their winters must be like. Then I thought, "What the heck? I might as well send a letter and a resumé." This would prove to be the best decision of my life, although at the time I considered it just another shot in the dark. Heavy-hearted, I made plans to move back to Bennettsville for what I hoped would be a short stay.

THEN AN EXCITING OPPORTUNITY lifted my spirits. On a whim, I had sent a tape of my playing to the South Carolina ETV Network, along with a biographical summary. Perhaps, I reasoned, a televised performance might attract the attention of a college or university in the Carolinas and prompt a job offer.

Imagine my surprise when an ETV executive wrote to me, saying they wanted me to prepare a half-hour program. He gave me the phone number of the ETV studio in Columbia and told me to call and set up a date for the taping. At a time when I badly needed a sense of direction, here was a project I could sink my teeth into.

PRIOR TO MY DEPARTURE from Champaign, Nancy Stagg and I went to our favorite Asian restaurant for a farewell dinner. I knew I would miss her terribly; we had been through so much together. Opening my fortune cookie, I read an intriguing prediction: "The position you desire will soon be yours." So it was—if fourteen months later can be considered *soon*.

AT THE END OF JUNE, Mother and Daddy arrived and loaded my belongings into a U-Haul trailer, bringing to a close a significant chapter of my life. In many ways, the past seven years had been unbelievably productive and rewarding. I had excelled as graduate student, dorm advisor, performer, and teacher. I had established my physical and emotional independence, forming friendships and associations that would last a lifetime. I tried to remain optimistic about the future but felt only a shroud of frustrating, agonizing uncertainty.

* * * * * *

ARRIVING IN BENNETTSVILLE, I contacted the ETV studio in Columbia, set up a date in late July for the taping of my recital, and immediately sought Fay McLaurin's advice in the selection of repertoire. These preparations were scarcely underway when Warren Scharf, Director of the Conservatory of Music at Baldwin Wallace College in Ohio, called to invite me to an interview. This was the job I had almost not applied for.

THE JOB AT BALDWIN WALLACE seemed promising in some respects. I learned that the core of my teaching load would be a beginning level course for non-piano music majors that combined group instruction in a Piano Lab with a short weekly private lesson. At UIUC, I had seen firsthand the benefits of piano classes, but had frequently wished for individual time with each student to work on specific problems. BW's system appealed to me, personally and pedagogically.

I felt discouraged and disheartened, however, when I saw the inaccessibility of the Conservatory building. What had once been an old freight elevator now served as a faculty mailroom. Someday, they said, a modern elevator would be installed, but no one could even estimate when that might be. To make matters worse, the second-floor Piano Lab could not be moved because of its specialized equipment and spatial requirements. They did say that I'd be given a studio on the second floor, so that all my teaching would take place on the same level. This concession lifted my spirits only slightly.

When I raised the accessibility issue, I was told that several music majors in wheelchairs had recently graduated from BW and that people had simply pitched in and carried them wherever they needed to go. I sighed, remembering how I had relied on the kindness of strangers to help me in and out of the old houses on Nevada Street at UIUC and realizing I would face a similar situation at BW. I seemed to encounter inaccessible facilities at every turn. Was finding a job in an accessible location too much to ask for?

Then came the perplexing disclosure that my chief competitor for the job was the person who currently held the position. In fact, about half of the music faculty favored retaining that person. My hopes instantly diminished; and as I expected, Warren Scharf called about a week after my interview to say that the "inside" candidate had been rehired for another year.

Disappointed but undeterred, I focused my attention on my upcoming television debut. Fay and I had chosen varied, listenable repertoire: Kabalevsky's *Variations in D Major*, two movements from Haydn's *Sonata in F Major*, a group of Schubert *German Dances*, and Chopin's *Nocturne in C-sharp Minor, Op. 27, No. 1*.

My director, Mike Brennan, approved the selections and told me to prepare spoken program notes about each piece: composer, title, and any historical or stylistic information I considered relevant. This format—talking, followed by playing—proved extremely effective and eventually became an integral feature of all my performances. A non-musician friend who saw my telecast remarked:"What strength comes from the spoken commentary! It provides a bridge straight from the keyboard to the audience."

The taping of my thirty-minute recital took eight hours. The first step, recording the sound, took about an hour. We spent the rest of the day on the visual aspects of the program. Various cameras filmed me from different angles as I played along with the tape. Trying to synchronize every nuance, so that the final product wouldn't look "faked," proved difficult and exhausting.

Whenever Mike yelled, "Kill the lights!" I could take a short break. After a few sips of water and a retouching of my makeup, our work would continue, and I do mean *work*. By the end of the day, feeling as limp as a dishrag, I had a healthy respect for what TV and movie actors have to endure to practice their craft. Perhaps with modern technology, the taping process would be easier today, but in 1975, it was almost as cumbersome and arduous as learning how to dress myself.

Mother and I were very pleased when we returned to Columbia several weeks later for an official preview of the program. Mike had done a skillful job of editing. In one or two places, the video was slightly out of sync with the audio, but these were scarcely noticeable and did not mar the performance. Mike had no idea when airtime might be, but promised to let us know the day and time.

BY THE END OF THE SUMMER, I had purchased a brand new, two-door, cranberry red Plymouth Fury. When I found a job, I was now ready to provide my own transportation—well, almost ready. I always entered and exited the car from the passenger side. I found that with my wheelchair nestled snugly behind the

Summer 1975: "Ready to roll"
in my new Plymouth Fury!

passenger seat, I could take it out of the car by myself, but I lacked the strength to lift the thirty-five-pound chair into the car. Daddy came to my rescue by recruiting two of his mechanically minded buddies to tackle the problem. Over a period of weeks, they worked with each other and with me to install a device suited to my needs and capabilities.

A piece of lightweight, strong "uniconstruct" was fastened to each interior side of the car just behind the front seats. It was two to three inches square and shaped like a "U." This "bar" was mounted with the slotted side down. The lips of the inverted "U" formed the track for two sets of nylon rollers fastened to a flat piece of metal, about eighteen to twenty-four inches in length, which telescoped into the track and could be pulled outside the car (when the door was open) to hook up the chair. At the end of the telescoping piece, a small hoist made of lightweight nylon cord, similar to those used on awnings, was mounted. A hook made out of a car radio antenna was fastened to the rope. The hook had two ends bent to slide under the chair armrests, one on each side.

In order to keep these two hooks in the proper location (so that the chair could be lifted in a normal position with wheels down), two everyday rubber hose clamps were positioned on each arm of the chair frame. Trial-and-error showed the proper location of these clamps.

The procedure was to fold the chair, pull out the telescoping piece, lower the hooks, place them between the clamps, then pull on the rope, which lifted the chair. The last step—pushing the telescoping piece back to its original position—secured the chair in its proper place.

Whenever possible, I took advantage of able-bodied help, but had peace of mind knowing that I could put the chair into the car by myself if I had to.

TWO VASTLY DIFFERENT OPPORTUNITIES kept me busy in the fall of 1975. Both allowed me to put my beautiful Fury to good use.

First, I agreed to serve as rehearsal accompanist for the local theater group's production of *The Sound of Music*, an assignment that required frequent trips to and from the Bennettsville High School Auditorium. After a few long evening rehearsals, I gave up practicing the score at home; I just showed up and sight-read whatever songs were on the agenda that night. The Fury needed some minor adjustments, and I recall driving to the dealership, sitting at the desk in the main office—manuscript paper spread around me—transposing *Edelweiss* to a lower key so that our Captain Von Trapp could sing it more comfortably.

I had signed on to be *rehearsal* accompanist, but when the music director decided to use the two-piano arrangement for the performances and wanted me to be one of the pianists, I could hardly refuse. Playing that 120-page score on three consecutive nights almost "did me in," however, the show was a huge hit, and I took great satisfaction in having been a part of its success.

Helen Rogers, my former St. Andrews faculty adviser, called me in early November to say that she had been ill for about a week. She wanted to stay home a few more days to regain her strength, but she feared her music theory classes were foundering in her absence. She asked if I might be willing to meet with the classes and help the students with their assignments. I considered this to be a labor of love. After all Helen had done for me, I wanted to return the favor in any way I could. Tutoring the students reinforced my dream of someday teaching full-time at a college or university.

DR. HORN, my first piano professor St. Andrews, had returned to the college in the mid-1970s. Both he and Helen knew of my performances at Illinois and urged me to play some of that repertoire at St. Andrews.

My guest recital on February 6, 1976, opened with the Alcalay *Two-Part Studies*, which I had premiered on my senior recital, followed by the Mozart, Chopin, and Bloch pieces from my 1969 UIUC recital. Scarcely two weeks later, I played the same program at Coker College in Hartsville, South Carolina. I had received this invitation through a Bennettsville native who was a piano major at Coker.

On March 16, the South Carolina ETV Network officially aired my recital (taped eight months earlier). Mother, Daddy, and I had to go to a friend's house to watch, because we didn't have cable TV. In the next three or four years, there were numerous unscheduled airings of my program. In fact, the network seems to have inserted it whenever a half-hour slot needed to be filled. My first piano teacher, Faye Griggs Bell (who had married and moved back to Bennettsville), wrote me that after seeing the show for the umpteenth time, she had grown a bit tired of it and would I please do a new one! My television exposure had no particular impact on my career, although it undoubtedly brought my playing to a much larger, more diverse audience than would ever have been able to hear me in person.

IN THE FOLLOWING MONTHS, WITH NO JOB PROSPECTS and no further performances, discouragement and boredom engulfed me. My three piano students and my participation in the choir at First United Methodist Church were definitely not enough to make me feel productive.

Badly in need of a little excitement and a change of scenery, I began planning an extensive trip in the Fury. I contacted friends in Richmond, Washington, D.C., and Philadelphia. All three said they'd love to have me come for a visit. I mapped the route thoroughly, making sure I'd have no more than about four hours of driving per day. In mid-May, I set out alone.

No mishaps marred my six-day excursion, although when I consider everything that could have gone wrong, my hair stands on end. After all, in 1976 there were no cell phones or GPS devices. I'm amazed that Mother and Daddy raised no objections, but I guess they figured their thirty-year-old daughter could make her own decisions.

BY JUNE, I FELT I HAD TO DO SOMETHING to secure my future. After consulting with Faye Griggs Bell and Fay McLaurin, I decided to set myself up in an independent piano studio in Columbia, South Carolina, a logical choice because of the city's size, resources, and relative proximity to Bennettsville (100 miles).

Preparations began in earnest. A cousin who lived in Columbia helped me find a suitable apartment. I located a piano teacher who had more students than she wanted and agreed to give me her overflow.

The next big step was the purchase of a piano. We still had an old upright at my parents' house, but I had always wanted a grand, and my Aunt Evelyn, Mother's older sister, had generously offered to fund the venture. Fay McLaurin went with me to Charlotte, North Carolina, where we tried out pianos at various dealerships. I selected a six-foot Kawai that remains one of my most prized possessions.

Mother and Daddy moved me into my Columbia apartment in late June. I eagerly awaited delivery of the Kawai, while Mother and I tended to details of furnishing and decorating. The apartment had a space specifically designated for a washer and dryer, but when I went shopping at Sears, only the dryer was in stock, so I told the sales representative I'd wait and make the purchase when both appliances were available. This proved to be a fateful and fortuitous circumstance.

A COLUMBIA HOTEL hosted the first Miss Wheelchair South Carolina pageant in mid-July. Since winning the title would bring valuable publicity to my studio, I thought I'd like to enter, but I worried there might be an age limit. The pageant coordinator assured me I wasn't too old. (I was thirty, but could easily have passed for eighteen or twenty.)

The director of the pageant turned out to be a silly, giggly woman whose total vocabulary consisted of three words: "Keep smiling, girls!" During the rehearsal, she tripped over an electrical cord and fell flat on her face. That sight kept smiles plastered on our faces for the remainder of the event.

My private interview with the judges dealt primarily with my disability and its effect on my personal and professional life. That evening, each contestant had to answer a question (drawn at random from a fishbowl) in front of the audience. I felt momentarily panic-stricken when I heard my question: "What would you do as Miss Wheelchair South Carolina to improve employment opportunities for the physically disabled?" I remember thinking, "How on earth can I respond to that question? I can't even find a job for myself!" After an awkward pause, I managed to say something, but this was not to be my crowning achievement. In fact, it belongs in that category of preposterous, embarrassing moments that are best forgotten. I don't recall my answer—only that the next thing I knew, my name was being called as one of the finalists.

The three of us were parked side by side on stage. When the girl on my left was named second runner-up, I thought momentarily that I might win. Then I took a good look at the girl on my right. Stunningly beautiful, she had been paralyzed from the neck down in some dreadful accident. Compared to her, I was able-bodied. I could hardly blame the judges for giving her the crown and naming me first runner-up.

Mother said I should have won. "If there had been a talent division," she added, "you definitely would have won."

I HAD BEGUN to feel comfortable in Columbia. My piano had been delivered and tuned. I had submitted an ad for my studio at the local newspaper. I had visited two churches and had been invited to join both congregations. I had received several inquiries from parents of prospective students, but had made no commitments. Every few days, I pestered the woman at Sears about the washer, only to be told, "No, it hasn't come in."

ONE AFTERNOON in early August, Mother called to say that she had given my Columbia phone number to Al Gay, Assistant Director of the Conservatory at Baldwin Wallace. When Dr. Gay reached me, his opening words were riveting: "Remember the job you interviewed for a year ago? If you're still interested, it's yours."

FACULTY RECITAL AT UNIVERSITY OF ILLINOIS

Great Hall
Krannert Center for the Performing Arts
Urbana, Illinois
February 20, 1975

Five Little Two-Voice Studies for Piano (1955) .... Lucia Alcalay
Andante
Allegro
Lento
Improvisando
Vivace

Sonata No. 38 in F Major (Hob. XVI: 23) .... Haydn
Moderato
Adagio
Finale – Presto

INTERMISSION

Four Mazurkas .... Chopin
B-flat Minor, Op. 24, No. 4
C Major, Op. 24, No. 2
A Minor, Op. 67, No. 4
A Minor, Op. 17, No. 4

Polonaise in C-sharp Minor, Op. 26, No. 1 .... Chopin

Nocturne in C Minor, Op. 48, No. 1 .... Chopin

Encore:
Etude in F Minor (from "Trois Nouvelles Etudes") .... Chopin

BALDWIN WALLACE—HERE I COME!

MY FIRST WORDS to Al Gay were: "What? Are you serious?" He was quite serious. The person who held the position had resigned for personal reasons.

My next question: "Will I have to be interviewed again?"

"No. We were very favorably impressed with you when you were here. If you want the job, you've got it. Simple as that."

Simple? My heart was pounding, my mind churning. When someone drops a bomb in your lap, the situation is not simple.

I finally managed to say, "Thank you. I'll give you an answer as soon as possible."

I called Mother right away. Remarkably calm, she offered her help and support, whatever I decided to do.

For the next forty-eight hours, my thoughts centered on the hardships I would face at Baldwin Wallace. I shuddered to think of the Conservatory building's inaccessibility. There were too many steps to negotiate manually; I'd have to be carried to and from the second floor every teaching day. The Northern Ohio winters presented another major concern. The marvelous Rehab bus service, which had met my transportation needs at UIUC, did not exist in the real world. I would undoubtedly have to drive my Fury in cold, snowy conditions. I could, of course, avoid these challenges by making the safe, conservative decision to remain in Columbia.

But—and this was a huge BUT—Mother had not raised me to

be safe and conservative. She had taken a huge leap of faith by signing me up for piano lessons in 1954. Over the years, my dream of teaching piano at the college level had gradually emerged. Now, at last, I had been given the opportunity to realize that dream. Yes, I had to go to Baldwin Wallace, face the challenges head on, and see firsthand what the difficulties and rewards might be.

I allowed myself the consoling thought that if things didn't work out at BW, I could return to Columbia and set up a studio anytime. I also realized there was no urgent reason for my staying in Columbia. I had made no commitments to students. I was not Miss Wheelchair South Carolina. I had not even purchased a washer and dryer.

I CALLED AL GAY AND ACCEPTED HIS OFFER. He immediately began detailing the nuts and bolts of the job. I would be hired as Instructor of Piano (the lowest academic rank), which seemed reasonable, given my paucity of previous experience and partially completed doctorate. My starting salary would be approximately $10,000 for the 1976-77 academic year. My first paycheck would be October 1. One of the Conservatory secretaries, Mrs. Ruth Donald, would apartment hunt for me. Ideally, I'd be moved in by September 1. Fall quarter classes started the third week of September.

Events of the next twenty-one days proceeded like clockwork. My landlord in Columbia allowed me to cancel my lease without penalty. Mrs. Donald found two apartments, both near the college. I chose, sight unseen, a one-bedroom unit at Tower in the Park, which, I learned, had a laundry room on each floor—no space for a washer and dryer in the apartment. This bit of information convinced me that going to BW was truly meant to be. I contacted the young man who had tuned my piano and asked if he'd move my piano to Ohio. He not only agreed, but also said he'd take my furniture in the same truck for the same price. Mother and I began repacking boxes.

On my last night in Columbia, I received a perfect send-off when Dean Sanders called to congratulate me and wish me well in my new job. Early the next morning, Mother and I loaded the Fury and headed for Ohio. My adventure in Columbia had ended abruptly. I had a feeling I would not be coming back.

CHAPTER NINE

SUCCESSFUL, BUT NOT INVINCIBLE

TOWER IN THE PARK stood at the entrance to the Cleveland Metroparks, the city's so-called "emerald necklace." The eight-story behemoth had three sprawling wings stretching east, west, and south. My apartment lay at the far end of the east wing. Both the living room balcony window and bedroom window overlooked a beautiful wooded area. I knew instantly that I had made a good choice.

Mother worked nonstop for three or four days getting me settled. After finally hanging the drapes just right, she remarked, "Vickie, please try to stay here at least a year or two. I don't think I can go through this very often." Having moved twice in two months, I wholeheartedly concurred.

Driving back to Berea after leaving Mother at the airport, I felt anxious and queasy. Although I had lived independently in Illinois, I had always been under the protective umbrella of the university. I now had a real job with potentially long-term professional responsibilities. Would I be able to "cut the mustard," as my daddy would say? Time would tell.

I QUICKLY LEARNED THE ADVANTAGES of living in a large apartment building as I became acquainted with a bevy of interesting, congenial people who were only an elevator ride away. Among the first to welcome me was Ruth Pickering from apartment 824. An avid amateur pianist, she had taught public school music in her younger years. Her husband, Don, was a psychology professor at BW. Their daughter, Jane, almost exactly my age, lived in Kentucky. Ruth and Don immediately took me under their wing and became my surrogate parents.

The Pickerings frequently hosted lively, entertaining "happy hours," where they presented me to their guests with great fanfare. Don would explain, "You know our daughter, Jane, but I'd like to introduce our *other* daughter, Vickie Covington." This would be followed by an in-depth recitation of my background and experience, concluding with my being "an outstanding new addition to BW's piano faculty."

I especially enjoyed meeting one of the Pickerings' favorite friends, Helen Wooley, a charming, cultured, well-educated woman, who also lived in the building. When Helen called to say she wanted to take Ruth, Don, and me out for dinner, I was thrilled, then puzzled as she added that the invitation carried a "condition." "Vickie," she said slyly, "you must promise me that you will order dessert. It always lifts my spirits just to watch you eat dessert!" Naturally, I had no problem making such a promise. That night, Don suggested that I try something new, Bananas Foster, which became my new favorite.

Ruth invited me to their apartment for dinner about once a week. I had grown up with my mother's Southern cooking, but quickly developed a taste for Ruth's Midwestern specialties: beef burgundy over rice, creamy turkey chowder, and cherry pie with made-from-scratch crust. I can work up an appetite just thinking about those delicious meals. Perfect gentleman that he was, Don always escorted me to and from my apartment, although in those days I could easily "push" myself down the hall in my manual wheelchair. "Save your energy for your teaching," he'd say with a laugh.

I FOLLOWED Don's excellent advice because in the fall quarter of 1976, I had fifty-one piano students: four sections of freshmen beginners (total enrollment of forty-one) and ten upperclassmen. The freshmen had three classes a week in the electronic Piano Lab and one fifteen-minute private weekly lesson in my studio. The upperclassmen had weekly half-hour private lessons. How I longed for my half-time teaching assignment at UIUC, which had involved a total of eight hours of instruction per week.

Since the piano labs met on Monday, Wednesday, and Friday, I scheduled as many private lessons as possible on those days. I used Tuesdays for "overflow" and makeup lessons. My four teaching days were long and strenuous, but I had Thursdays and the weekend for R and R.

The four-day week also eased the requirements of getting me to and from the second floor of the Conservatory building. A handicapped parking space had been reserved for me near the entrance. Warren Scharf, the Conservatory Director, arranged for a senior music major to meet me at my car each morning. The student then located a second able-bodied person to help with the hoisting and lifting necessary to get me up the stairs in my chair. In the afternoon I was on my own, but generally had no problem locating sturdy volunteers. This routine, with minor variations and adjustments, remained the same throughout my first *ten years* at BW.

No system is flawless or foolproof. Although I sometimes felt frustrated, if not downright angry, that getting from Point A to Point B was so complicated, the sympathetic, cooperative people around me made this less-than-ideal situation tolerable. I managed, for the most part, to retain my sanity.

One afternoon, arriving at my apartment after a particularly long, difficult, hectic day, I found a note from Ruth tucked under the door: "Call me when you've finished dinner. I'll bring you a serving of Bananas Foster for dessert."

THE CONSERVATORY'S PROXIMITY to Tower in the Park (one mile) made for an easy drive in good weather; in nasty weather, I could at least be grateful for the short distance. About midway through fall quarter, I realized that when winter arrived, a parking garage would be a necessity. Without it, I'd have to hire someone to dig the Fury out of the snow. As it turned out, I had to rent a double garage space in order to have enough room to open the passenger door wide and put my chair into the car. Moreover, I learned that I couldn't rent the garage just for the winter; I had to sign a year's lease. What choice did I have? I agreed to the terms, concluding that the money was well spent.

One day in October, I stopped at the Sohio station where I bought gas to ask about snow tires. When the attendant quoted me the price per tire and gave me the total amount, I said, "But that's for only two."

His amused response: "Lady, you don't have a lot of experience buying snow tires, do you?" Thank goodness for his honesty. I would have bought four tires and not batted an eyelash.

When I had called Al Gay to accept the job, he assured me that Berea winters were not that bad. "We have only a few weeks of heavy snow," he had said, or words to that effect. In 1976, however, the first measurable snow came before the end of October. As the white stuff piled up, I began to have serious doubts about Al Gay's honesty. People kept telling me how unusual it was to have so much snow, so early in the season, but these observations gave me no comfort. *Snow*, I concluded, is definitely a four-letter word.

It took me a minimum of ten to fifteen minutes to push from the apartment building to my garage in strong wind and heavy snow. The maintenance crew at Tower in the Park generally kept walkways clear, but one morning in January, as I rounded the corner to my carport, I got stuck in the snow. "Spinning my wheels," I couldn't move either forward or backward.

I heard a voice behind me: "Do you need help?"

The voice belonged to a very pleasant-looking man who easily dislodged me from the snow and whisked me to my car. He wanted to know my destination.

"Baldwin Wallace."

"Oh, are you a new student?

"No, I'm a new faculty member."

"Oh!" He seemed surprised and a bit incredulous.

About a week later, I got stuck in the snow again. The same kindly stranger rescued me, although now he didn't seem like a stranger.

After our third encounter, he quipped, "We have to stop meeting like this." We proceeded to introduce ourselves. He was Ray Kubacki, a professional photographer at a local studio, who had recently moved into apartment 427. He gave me his telephone number, adding that he would gladly help me to my car on a regular basis since, as he put it, "We both seem to be leaving for work about the same time every morning." I valued my independence, but in this case, I had to be practical and realistic. Ray's assistance could save me a lot of time and energy, so I called him and gratefully accepted his offer.

I quickly discovered Ray's wholehearted devotion to his family, including his ex-wife, who had divorced him six months earlier. Of their seven children, the two youngest (teenagers) were still at home Ray told me later that knowing me gave him the incentive to lift himself out of his "pity party" and put his life back together.

Ray had never cooked during his married years, but before long, he was treating me to sumptuous fare almost every Sunday night—his way of fortifying me for the week ahead. "You're such a skinny little kid," he'd say, "you need all the nourishment you can get."

IN 1976, BW HAD FOUR FULLTIME PIANO FACULTY MEMBERS. Evelyn Gott and George Cherry were tenured professors. Robert Mayerovitch, a young Canadian pianist, and I were the new recruits. Evelyn was serving a three-year term as department head, a rotating position at BW. Both she and George welcomed me enthusiastically, taking great pains to acquaint me with the workings of the department, as well as the specific proficiency skills that would be required of my students at each level of study. George's wife, Lynne, also a fine pianist and frequently his piano duet partner, endeared herself to me right away by locating a small local grocery store that provided delivery service. In later years, when my health failed, Lynne would earn her stripes by taking over a portion of my teaching load.

Evelyn, George, Bob, and Lynne became my closest colleagues, as well as trusted friends. We coalesced into an effective team, meeting regularly, discussing issues and problems openly, and generally resolving differences amicably. At UIUC, the Group Piano faculty had been relegated to a separate department. Happily, this was not the case at BW. Although in the beginning, I taught only piano minors, I always felt like a fully functioning member of the department, never a second-class citizen.

Outside the piano department, my favorite colleague was Dr. James Feldman, professor of music theory—a phenomenal teacher, an excellent pianist, and an extraordinary man. His dry, clever wit made him a delightful conversationalist; his mild, self-deprecating manner cloaked his brilliant intelligence.

Jim's incomparable prose strengthened all of my applications for promotion and tenure at BW. He once described me as "a redoubtable blend of geniality, integrity, and munificence" and called my playing "eloquent and poetic . . . not one note goes uncherished. Seated at the keyboard, she divines truths wedged in the crannies of a swarming world." These lofty sentiments both inspired and humbled me. Jim suffered an untimely death from ALS a few years ago, but his legacy lives on in everyone who knew him.

My friendship with Jim began shortly after my arrival in Berea when he went with me to the DMV office to have my driver's license transferred to Ohio. Daddy had arranged for the transfer of my Illinois license to South Carolina with one phone call to a friend of his. I had no such luck in Cleveland. I was told I'd have to take a driving test, including parallel parking, a skill that had not been required for my license in Illinois. Dismayed over this unexpected roadblock (pun intended), I immediately thought, "Would they require an able-bodied licensed driver to take a road test?" I probably should have asked that very question, but I didn't. I just said I'd return at a later date after I had mastered parallel parking.

As the weeks and months went by and the challenges of my job mounted, parallel parking seemed less and less important. So for the next twelve years, using my parents' address, I simply renewed my South Carolina license. At last, in March 1988, the auto insurance company sent me a letter pointing out that I was driving with an out-of-state license, as if I were not aware of this already. At that point, I had decided to sell my car, hire a driver, and let my license expire. Everything worked out fine, and I never had to endure the agony of learning to parallel park.

BALDWIN WALLACE is justifiably renowned as the site each spring of the oldest collegiate-sponsored Bach Festival in the United States. J.S. Bach's four major choral works, the *St. Matthew Passion*, *St. John Passion*, *Christmas Oratorio*, and *Mass in B*

Minor, are presented on a rotating basis along with other repertoire by Bach and his contemporaries. Professional singers perform solo roles, while the festival orchestra and chorus are made up entirely of BW students and faculty.

I invited my UIUC friend, Nancy Stagg, to join me for my first festival in May 1977. Of course, she insisted on an in-depth report of my BW experiences, which I happily provided, in between concerts.

In stark contrast to the joy of Nancy's visit was a letter from Phyllis Goren's mother, saying that Phyllis had been moved to a Denver nursing home. Mrs. Goren gave me Phyllis's telephone number and asked me to call her. With a heavy heart, I complied. I could barely hear the weak, tentative voice at the other end of the line, but I could sense her excitement about my job. We spoke for only a few minutes. As soon as I hung up, I burst into tears. A few weeks later, I learned that Phyllis had died.

NEVER HAVE I WORKED AS HARD as I did my first year at BW. The combination of group and private instruction for the freshmen beginners made my job both easier and harder: easier, because I could work with each individual on specific problems; harder, because the private lessons were only fifteen minutes. Seeing four students in an hour is definitely more labor-intensive than an hour-long lesson with just one student.

Although my students were not piano majors, they were music majors. Most of them understood that pianistic skills would be crucial to their ultimate success in the professional world. Many of my students told me, "I've always wanted to learn to play the piano. I'm so glad to have this opportunity." Of course, the talented students were a pleasure to teach and made rapid progress. My greatest satisfaction, however, came from those who were less gifted, but nevertheless excelled due to consistent effort and, in some cases, sheer determination.

As the end of spring quarter approached, I awaited eagerly and somewhat nervously the day when my young charges would be taking their proficiency exams. The requirements included a piece of prepared repertoire, sight-reading, and harmonization of a melody (at sight) using specified chord progressions. The proficiencies took the form of "juries," with the piano faculty serving as the jury. I would be present for my students' juries, but the other members of the faculty would vote and render the verdict.

Most of my students passed, but there were a few disappointments, for which I tended to blame myself. Surely, if I had done things differently, the outcome would have been positive. Even after years of experience, I never quite overcame a personal sense of failure whenever my students didn't make the grade.

Shortly before leaving for summer vacation in South Carolina, I found the following anonymous note taped to my studio door. It instantly lifted my spirits and renewed my optimism for the future:

> *Miss Covington has been the best piano teacher I have ever had. She can understand where the students are having difficulty and usually knows what to suggest to fix the problem. She has been very helpful and never makes one feel out of place even if the person needs extra attention or help. I have recommended her to other students.*
>
> *Miss Covington is a tremendous asset to the BW Conservatory.*
>
> *I hope others have benefited as much as I have.*

I spent most of the summer preparing for my first faculty recital at Baldwin Wallace, scheduled for October. Knowing I would feel pressured and nervous, I decided to play the same repertoire that had served me well on my guest recitals at St. Andrews and Coker: Alcalay, Mozart, Chopin, and Bloch.

I luxuriated in the prospect of performing again. I had completed only one year of fulltime teaching, yet I already felt the tug-of-war between my teaching responsibilities and my own need for artistic expression. This conflict—familiar to many artists, writers, and musicians who work in academic settings—was new to me. With a rather rude awakening, I thought, "This is the real world, and I'd better get used to it."

MY SISTER MARY JO, who had been living with our recently widowed Aunt Evelyn in Warwick, Rhode Island, was about to graduate with a degree in textiles from the university there. Through the years, I had not seen Aunt Evelyn often, so her invitation for me to fly to Rhode Island for a week in late July was a pleasant surprise. I also welcomed the opportunity to spend some quality time with Mary Jo.

My enjoyable visit included excursions with Mary Jo to the sites of the area, as well as a trip to New York City, where we viewed historical musical instruments at the Metropolitan Museum of Art and attended one of Yul Brenner's last performances in *The King and I* on Broadway. I did indeed have the chance to get better acquainted with Aunt Evelyn who, for much of my life, had been a benevolent stranger. I told her about my job, my new friends and colleagues, and how much I loved my Kawai grand piano, which her generosity had enabled me to purchase. I never saw Aunt Evelyn again. She died of cancer five years later.

MY RECITAL of October 8, 1977, was well attended and enthusiastically received. Mother and Daddy drove from

Bennettsville (Daddy's only trip to Berea); Mary Jo came from Madison, Wisconsin, where she had gotten a job. As I took my final bow, one of my students came onstage with a beautiful bouquet of flowers. I learned later that my students had taken up a collection to buy it for me.

Ray Kubacki served as official photographer for the event. After the performance, the Pickerings hosted a small reception at their apartment. Among the guests were Dean Neal Malicky and Assistant Conservatory Director, Al Gay, along with their wives. This successful, memorable evening made me feel that Baldwin Wallace just might become my home.

THE MID-1970s were also banner years for Mother. Her South Carolina tennis rankings had soared to number one in three categories—35 doubles, 45 singles, and 45 doubles. In the South, she was ranked number-one in women's 55 singles and women's 60 singles and doubles. In 1977, she held sixth place nationally in women's 55 singles. With the addition of older age brackets, she noted wryly that now "at least some provision is being made for old ladies like me who are crazy enough to play in tournaments."

AS BAD AS MY FIRST WINTER AT BW HAD BEEN, my second was even worse—with a total seasonal snowfall of well over 100 inches, more than twice the normal amount. The severity of one storm prompted the college to take the highly unusual step of canceling classes for several days. When spring arrived, there were T-shirts proclaiming, "I Survived the Blizzard of '78!"

Ray continued to be my guardian angel. On severely cold mornings, instead of pushing me to my carport, he'd leave me in the lobby while he went to get the Fury. Often I'd watch as he seemed to disappear into a swirl of snow. In a few minutes, he'd drive the Fury as close to the building as he could. After helping me into the driver's seat and putting my chair in its accustomed spot, he'd give me a kiss on the cheek, admonish me to "be careful," and off I'd go.

How did a Southern girl like me learn to drive in the snow? You don't learn to do it. You just do it—cautiously, slowly, prayerfully. I was now convinced that Al Gay had lied (albeit unintentionally) about the Berea winters. He eventually confessed to me, "Vickie, it was at least three years before I could look you in the eye!"

WITH MY PROMOTION to the rank of assistant professor in the spring of 1978, my position at BW seemed somehow more permanent. I had read in the faculty handbook that promotions to associate professor required "an earned doctorate or its equivalent." I was always thinking ahead. Equivalency meant establishing a national reputation in one's field through performing, lecturing, publishing, etc. Since I might never achieve this status (and if I did, certainly not within the foreseeable future), an "earned doctorate" offered the most realistic path for securing my professional future. Simply put—I would have to bite the bullet and finish my Ed.D., the degree I had unceremoniously abandoned in 1974.

Now that my perspective and outlook had changed completely, I decided to call Dr. Leonhard and ask whether or not he would support my reinstatement into the music education doctoral program. His answer: "Absolutely!"

I attended four consecutive summer school sessions at the University of Illinois, beginning in June 1978. As usual, Mother took over the mechanics of moving. As soon as my school year ended at BW, she flew to Cleveland. We loaded the Fury, and she drove us to Champaign (about eight hours). After spending two or three days getting me settled in my efficiency apartment, the same building where I had lived from 1973-75, she flew back to South Carolina.

At the conclusion of summer school, we reversed the procedure. Mother flew to Champaign. We loaded the Fury and made the drive to Cleveland. After unpacking everything, we both flew to South Carolina, where I'd have about two weeks of vacation before flying back to Cleveland for the start of another teaching year. Mother expended enormous amounts of time, energy, and money during this period. More than once, she'd say jokingly, "Remember, when you get your doctorate, a little piece of it belongs to me!"

Whenever people tell me how smart I was to complete advanced degrees, I say, "You don't have to be *smart*; you have to be *persistent*." This is especially true at the doctoral level. One simply has to jump through all the hoops in the prescribed order, within the prescribed time frame. Having a cooperative, influential adviser like Dr. Leonhard helps tremendously.

First, I had to retake the portion of the qualifying examination I had failed, so I spent my first summer session devouring everything I could get my hands on dealing with current issues in music education. Since the exam took place on the last day of summer school, I left campus not knowing the outcome. Within a couple of weeks, I received a letter informing me that I had passed. I was now "qualified" to develop a thesis proposal. Vacillating between joy and dread, I resolutely focused on the positive: I had made it through another hoop.

AFTER LEAVING ST. ANDREWS in 1969, Dady Mehta spent the rest of his career at Eastern Michigan University in Ypsilanti. In addition, he taught several summers at Interlochen, Michigan's famous music camp for young students. At the end of August 1978, Interlochen hosted an *adult* music week. Dady had agreed to conduct a master class for piano teachers, but he called me in something of a panic because he had learned that most of the teachers who had enrolled in the class wanted to observe, not perform.

"If you come visit us, you can play in my class every day," he reasoned. "That will surely inspire some of the observers to participate." I had been single-mindedly focused on my exam—piano practicing was a distant memory. However, my faculty recital pieces from 1977 were still more or less "under my fingers," so I said, "Sure, count me in."

Daily classes and lectures, as well as nightly concerts, provided a stimulating week of total immersion in the musical process. Dady played a stunning solo recital, which included my favorite Schubert sonata. Afterward, he wanted to know my reactions and opinions about his performance. "How exciting!" I thought. "He's treating me more like a colleague than a former student." I felt I had *arrived*.

My Interlochen experience led to an interesting postscript. Paul Statsky, a violin instructor at the Interlochen Arts Academy, heard me play in Dady's classes and decided he'd like us to be partners in a program. (My Baldwin Wallace association had also caught his attention because of his friendship with BW's violin professor.) Dady helped us select suitable repertoire by Corelli, Mozart, Schumann, and Schubert, which Paul and I performed at BW on April 7, 1979, and in Bennettsville—under the auspices of the Marlboro Arts Council—the following August. I never again had the opportunity to play chamber music, although I found my experience with Paul both stimulating and satisfying.

DURING THE SUMMER of 1979, Dr. Leonhard and I fine-tuned the proposal for my dissertation: "Approaches To Piano Reading in a Selected Sample of Current Instructional Materials For Adult

Beginners." The cumbersome title belied a relatively straight-forward purpose: to describe approaches to the development of sight-reading skills in the ten instructional books being used most frequently at the college/university level in the teaching of beginning adult piano students. The sample would be determined through a mail survey of class piano chairmen at 137 schools across the country. The fact that most of my BW students were adult beginners made this a relevant, timely topic for me.

My master's thesis had taken shape as the project unfolded, but for the doctoral document, I had to explain organization and detail upfront. Once completed and approved, the proposal functioned like a contract, stating precisely what I would do as well as when and how I would do it.

Doctoral candidates were required to take a preliminary examination—an oral defense of the dissertation proposal and procedures with members of the doctoral committee. After passing this exam, the student could begin work on the dissertation. Since I did not complete my proposal until the very end of summer school, there was insufficient time to assemble the committee and schedule the exam. I asked Dr. Leonhard what I should do. He said simply, "There's no need for you to make another trip here this fall to satisfy a formality, so don't worry about it. I'll collect the committee's signatures and do the necessary paperwork." Just like that—with a wave of his magic wand—he had eliminated one of my doctoral requirements. Sure enough, in a few weeks the Graduate Music Office sent me a letter saying that I had "passed" my preliminary exam.

By mid-October, I had completed the mail survey and purchased the books that would comprise my sample (several of which I already owned); but for the remainder of the school year, I accomplished very little toward the dissertation. At BW, my teaching came first. Only in the summer did I wear a student hat.

A TERRIBLE COLD AND COUGH PLAGUED ME throughout my Christmas vacation in South Carolina. I foolishly did not seek medical attention. As winter quarter began at the college, my condition worsened. One morning, I felt a sharp pain in my right rib cage. Ray took me to a doctor, who diagnosed me with bronchitis and a bruised rib (from excessive coughing). He prescribed an antibiotic, then advised me get a vaporizer and rest until the rib healed.

Upon learning of my predicament, Mother boarded the next flight to Cleveland. When Ray met her at the airport and saw the large case on her arm, he assumed it was her luggage. "Oh, no," she corrected him. "This is just the food." She had taken steaks, homemade vegetable soup, and other items from her home freezer and had brought them with her in a cooler.

I recall vividly her coming into the bedroom, rushing over to me, kissing me on the forehead, and saying, "How's my little girl?"

I think I responded, between coughs, "Rather puny."

After three or four days of delicious, nutritious meals and plenty of TLC, I had recovered nicely. Mother flew back to South Carolina, leaving a variety of home-cooked goodies in my freezer. Once again, she had demonstrated her readiness and willingness to rescue me from any difficulty, whenever and however she could.

OUT OF THE BLUE, the president of the Bennettsville Pilot Club, an organization for business and professional women, contacted me in February with the startling news that the group wanted to nominate me for their 1980 Handicapped Professional Woman of the Year award. I quickly assembled biographical information and letters of recommendation. At the club's March meeting, which conveniently fell during my spring break, I received an engraved Jefferson cup and made a brief acceptance speech. In attendance were my parents and my first two piano teachers, Faye Griggs Bell and Fay McLaurin.

The local nomination automatically made me a contender for the state award, which I won. On April 26, I flew from Cleveland to Augusta, Georgia, for the Pilot Club's regional convention. When Daddy met me at the airport by himself, I knew instantly that something must be wrong with Mother. She had been hospitalized in Bennettsville with hepatitis! Daddy gave me this handwritten note:

Dearest Vickie,

I want you to play just a little extra well tonight for "dear ol' Mom," who wishes she could be there where all the excitement is!

Best wishes in your speech and playing. I am so proud of you.
Dearest love,
Mother

At the banquet that night, I had to make the best of a decidedly unfriendly piano, but the Chopin *C-sharp Minor Nocturne* was, as always, a hit with the audience. My speech and my performance drew standing ovations. Only Mother's absence marred the thrill of the occasion. Fortunately, within a week, she had fully recovered.

Shortly after my return to Cleveland, a reporter from the BW newspaper appeared at my studio to interview me about my recent award and take my picture. I welcomed the interview, but strenuously protested the picture. I had worn my Bach Festival T-shirt that day, hardly suitable attire for a faculty photo. The young man would not take "no" for an answer, so I reluctantly agreed, thinking that the story would probably be buried in some unnoticeable spot and that maybe they wouldn't even use the picture. No such luck.The next issue of the paper featured a huge front-page headline: AWARD BESTOWED ON PIANO PROFESSOR. The picture showed me seated at the piano in my studio, wearing my T-shirt, looking (according to my colleagues) like a teenager.

DURING THE SUMMER OF 1980, I wrote a dreadfully tedious chapter of my dissertation, "A Review of Related Litera-ture," which required that I spend many hours in the music library, poring over books, articles, and dissertations on subjects that were related in some way to my topic. Although Dr. Leonhard allowed me to consult dissertation abstracts—where I could see at a glance the premise, procedures, and conclusions of each document—the process was still arduous, and the finished chapter deadly dull. I decided that the only possible use for this chapter would be as a cure for insomnia, since reading more than two or three pages would surely induce deep sleep.

By August, I realized that I would need one more year to complete the dissertation. I set my sights on the fall of 1981. The date, exactly ten years after I had received my master's degree, seemed somehow appropriate.

MARTIN COX, who was still my favorite bus driver, had heard of my mother's tennis skills and knew she'd be flying to Champaign at the end of summer school to help me move back to Ohio. Martin had hatched a scheme involving a rehab center employee, Mr. Woodbine [not his real name], a tennis swell-head who badly needed a lesson in humility. One day Martin asked me a loaded question: "Do you to think your mother could challenge Mr Woodbine to a tennis match and beat the crap out of him?"

"What a splendid idea!" I responded. "She could probably do just that."

The match was arranged, and the appointed day arrived. Since

Mother seemed a bit nervous, I offered to go with her, but she said that would only make her more nervous. I tried to be soothing: "Just do the best you can, Mother. I'm sure that's all Martin expects."

"No," she insisted. "You said Martin wants me to beat the crap out of this guy, and that's what I intend to do!" This was a woman on a mission.

After Mother left, I settled in to revise a particularly boring section of my dissertation. Scarcely an hour later, she returned, grinning broadly.

"Don't just stand there—tell me what happened," I said.

"Well, we played two sets, and Mr. Woodbine didn't win a single game. In the second set, I started to let him win a game or two, but then I'd think about Martin, and that would inspire me to put away another backhand winner." She added that Mr. Woodbine, embarrassed and exhausted, had refused her offer to play a third set.

The next day, as I boarded Martin's bus, I proclaimed, "Mission accomplished" and filled in the juicy details. "I love it—I love it!" he laughed loudly. "Give your mother a big hug for me." I promised I would.

Martin and Mother never met, but a strong bond was forged between them that fateful day in August 1980. Martin couldn't have been happier about Mother's induction into the South Carolina Tennis Hall of Fame in 1994 and the Furman University Athletic Hall of Fame in 1995. And at least poor Mr. Woodbine had the consolation of knowing he'd been beaten by the best.

In addition to Mr. Woodbine's comeuppance, the summers of 1978-81 provided other opportunities for fun and frolic. Nancy Stagg had bought a house in Urbana and was proving herself to be indispensable to the local National Public Radio station. Her June birthday usually coincided with Mother's and my arrival on campus, so we made it our custom to take her out for a celebratory dinner. Throughout the summer, Nancy and I chatted by phone and enjoyed various outings. "Call me whenever you come up for air!" she'd say, and I knew she meant it.

I also reconnected with my former piano teachers, Tom Baker and Dean Sanders. Tom had returned to UIUC to finish his Doctor of Musical Arts in Piano Performance. Although none of his solo recitals were in the summer, I did have the pleasure of hearing him accompany a soprano who was completing her DMA. Dean always invited me to his home for a lovely dinner on the patio. Both Tom and Dean were ecstatic over my success at Baldwin Wallace and wanted a blow-by-blow account of my experiences.

At the close of each summer school session, Mother and I attended Dr. Leonhard's annual poolside party for graduate students and their spouses/guests. Everyone enjoyed seeing his elegant house and gorgeous Persian cats as well as re-hashing the accomplishments of the summer. Mother's assessment of Dr. Leonhard: "He tries to act tough, but he's really a big Teddy Bear."

BY MID-JULY 1981, my 200-page "masterpiece" was typed and ready to be submitted to the other members of my doctoral committee, Dr. Richard Colwell and Dr. G. David Peters, both music education professors at UIUC. Dr. Leonhard had consistently expressed satisfaction with my work, but I needed unanimous committee approval in order for my dissertation to be accepted. I would have to meet with the committee to defend my dissertation orally. This requirement could not be bypassed or dismissed as a formality. Dr. Colwell's presence on the committee made me nervous because he had a reputation for being difficult and a stickler for detail. What if he insisted on extensive revisions and changes? Might the conferring of my degree be delayed? The potential complications seemed endless.

I saw Dr. Leonhard in the hallway of the music building the day before my oral defense and told him I was going back to my apartment to do some last-minute studying.

"No," he said emphatically. "Take a friend out for dinner. Go to a movie. Read a good novel. Do whatever you want to do, but don't study and don't worry." I tried to follow his advice. I didn't study, but I couldn't help wondering from time to time what Dr. Colwell might have up his sleeve.

The next day, my stomach in knots, I entered the room where the committee had gathered. Dr. Leonhard's opening remarks blew me away: "I'd like to begin by saying a few words about this remarkable woman. Whenever I feel discouraged or disheartened, I think of Vickie Covington and all that she has accomplished, all that she has overcome. Her courage is a constant source of inspiration to me. I am immensely proud of her work and proud to have had a role in her professional development."

I went into shock. I could feel that my cheeks were hot and flushed, yet cold chills engulfed the rest of my body. I suddenly realized that in singling me out for special praise, Dr. Leonhard had declared me his fair-haired child. "God" himself had given me his blessing; the "lesser deities" would not do or say anything to overrule him. I was home free. There were, in fact, numerous recommended revisions to my dissertation, mostly from Colwell, but nothing substantive, nothing that my typist couldn't handle easily. Yes, I was home free.

At the end of the session, Drs. Leonhard, Colwell, and Peters passed around and signed multiple copies of the official form that signified acceptance of my dissertation "in fulfillment of the requirements for the degree of Doctor of Education in Music Education." I sat there smiling, absorbing the joy, relief, and satisfaction of the moment.

After all the copies had been signed, I found myself saying

impulsively, "Dr. Leonhard, could you sign an extra one for my mother?"

"Absolutely! Let's sign an extra one for Vickie's mother."

I spent the rest of the day on the phone, sharing my spectacular news with my friends—but, of course, I called Mother first.

THE NECESSARY REVISIONS to my dissertation took longer than anticipated, so when I brought the final draft to the Graduate Music Office for format check (to make sure margins, footnotes, musical examples, etc., were spaced properly), I was dismayed to learn the process would require three days. I didn't have three days. The summer lease on my apartment expired in two days, and Mother and I had to drive back to Ohio in order to catch a plane to South Carolina.

One last time, I went to Dr. Leonhard for a favor. Perfectly calm and matter-of-fact, he said, "I'll tell the secretary to have your dissertation ready tomorrow morning." So, with literally moments to spare, I had my dissertation printed and distributed copies to the appropriate offices.

On the way to Cleveland, I remarked to Mother: "Next summer I can actually choose what I want to do, because I *won't* be working on my doctorate. Yay!"

WE FOUND A HUGE BANNER draped over the door of my apartment at Tower in the Park: "Congratulations & Welcome Back, DOCTOR VICTORIA COVINGTON!" Ruth and Don Pickering were the responsible parties. Everyone I knew in the building, plus a few people whose names I didn't recognize, had attached their signatures.

Back in South Carolina, the celebrations continued as I eagerly spread the glad tidings. One of my UIUC classmates called long distance, person-to-person for "Doctor Victoria Covington." I rather liked this new title. I visited my former St. Andrews professors, Herbert Horn and Helen Rogers, who obviously could appreciate the significance of the doctorate in solidifying my future at Baldwin Wallace.

As the 1981-82 academic year started, I received a shocking letter from Dr. Horn. Helen had been found dead in her yard, apparently having suffered a massive heart attack. She had retired from teaching, but had seemed in good health. Despite my overwhelming sense of loss, I took some comfort from the fact that at least I had been able to tell her in person about my doctorate and to thank her for her support and encouragement through the years.

My BW colleagues rejoiced with me over my latest accomplishment and were probably secretly relieved that I could now devote myself to duties at the college unfettered by the distractions and pressures of the doctorate. Feeling light as a feather, free as a breeze, I began planning and doing everything I had put on hold during the past three years. Unfortunately, I did not foresee that my excessive zeal and enthusiasm would ultimately damage my health and irreparably impair my body's immune system.

FOR MY SOLO FACULTY RECITAL on April 3, 1982 (my first since '77), I assembled a program of repertoire I had played on various occasions at Illinois: Krenek's *Eight Piano Pieces*, Haydn's *F Major Sonata*, five Chopin mazurkas, and two Chopin nocturnes. Returning to the format that had enhanced my ETV appearance, I prepared spoken commentary for each group of pieces. The positive feedback I received reassured me that my information and insights had been meaningful to the musicians in the audience without going over the heads of non-musicians.

Mark Collier, BW's new dean (and future president), attended the recital and sent me the following memo on April 7:

> *Dear Vickie,*
>
> *Just a note to tell you how very, very much I enjoyed your recital. I was impressed by the variety of music you performed and by the helpfulness and warmth of your interpretive comments. Most of all, I was almost overwhelmed by your artistry at the piano.*
>
> *This is yet another example of why I am so pleased that you are a part of the BW community. In so many ways, you exemplify this college at its best.*
> *Very sincerely,*
> *Mark*

In a letter dated just twelve days later, Mark informed me that the Board of Trustees had approved my application for tenure. The significance of this milestone can hardly be overestimated. Tenure, which is granted or denied at the end of one's sixth year following a comprehensive evaluation, essentially means job security for life, barring gross incompetence or misconduct on the part of the faculty member or the financial collapse of the school. Denial of tenure results in the dreaded seventh-year contract, which says, in effect, "Pack your bags and start job hunting." Thankfully, I would not be doing that.

Ruth and Don sent me a congratulatory note: "Tenure—what a good sound! Joy, joy, joy! We're so happy for you and for all of us."

DEPARTMENTAL HEADSHIPS at the Conservatory were three-year terms that rotated among full-time members of each department. With the end of Bob Mayerovitch's term in the spring of 1982, I knew my term would begin in September. I accepted the added responsibilities with some fear and trembling, but did not consider declining the appointment, even though I knew my teaching load would not be reduced and there would be no additional financial compensation. Despite my misgivings, I welcomed the opportunity to prove myself a fully functioning member of the department.

Dr. Ringer, my master's thesis advisor, sent me these confident, encouraging words:

So, you are Madam Chairman of the Piano Department. It couldn't have happened to a better-qualified person. Congratulations to you, as well as to Baldwin Wallace. I am sure it is a lot of work. I have no doubt, though, that you are getting a kick out of trying to get others to do things your way. Your public relations were always good, and I am not worried a bit along those lines.

Believing that I was invincible, I launched two huge additional projects during the summer of 1982. First, I decided to have my teeth straightened, after learning that the total cost of the venture would be almost exactly the amount I had recently inherited from Aunt Evelyn. The process began with oral surgery in June for the removal of four existing teeth and two impacted wisdom teeth. About a month later, my orthodontist fitted me with braces. Thus began two and a half years of monthly orthodontic adjustments. I never regretted straightening my teeth, as the benefits far outweighed the pain and inconvenience, but I should have delayed this undertaking until the conclusion of my term as department head. I discovered the hard way the truth of the old saying about hindsight.

When not dealing with my teeth, I busied myself with the selection of new solo repertoire, focusing on two composers whose music I loved and admired: Mozart and Chopin. Despite their short life spans (thirty-five and thirty-nine years, respectively), both grew and matured tremendously during their compositional careers. Offering a sample of their early and late works would, I thought, make an effective contrast and provide interesting material for spoken commentary.

First, I decided to pair Mozart's light, pleasant *Sonata in C Major, K. 279* with the dramatic, powerful, almost romantic *Adagio in B Minor, K. 540*. Hearing the juxtaposition of the two works, the listener might well have trouble believing they were written by the same composer.

For the opening Chopin segment, I chose two contrasting nocturnes, neither of which I had ever studied or played before. Four mazurkas comprised the final group: the first three being relatively typical, while the last one, among the longest and most complex of these dances, features canonic imitation (melodic lines that imitate each other), a rare occurrence in Chopin and a testament to his adulation of J.S. Bach. As an encore, I chose Chopin's famous and familiar *Nocturne in E-flat Major, Op. 9, No. 2*.

Although anxious to learn and memorize this music, I had to put recital preparations on a back burner when the school year began in mid-September. My full-time teaching load, regular orthodontic appointments, and especially my new administrative duties gave me little, if any, room to breathe.

Dr. Ringer knew whereof he spoke. Being Madam Chairman involved a lot of work. I had expected to be responsible for routine departmental business and correspondence; I had not anticipated the deluge of detail that confronted me. Every special request and every form needing a signature came across my desk. At the end of each academic quarter, I had to organize and distribute the jury (final exam) schedule for piano majors and minors. Held during Exam Week, juries ranged in length from five minutes (piano minor beginners) to twenty minutes (piano majors). Any student needing to change or cancel a jury had to see the department head.

In 1982, with enrollments declining, all departments in the Conservatory were being pressured to recruit, recruit, recruit. Brainstorming over a period of weeks, my colleagues and I gradually developed a plan for an annual workshop, free for any high school pianist wishing to attend, to be held on the second Saturday in February. The morning would begin with informal lessons in piano faculty studios, followed by lunch and a campus tour with BW music majors. Short performances by one or two of our best piano majors would jump-start the afternoon session in the large auditorium. To conclude the day, chairs would be arranged in a circle onstage for an open discussion of careers in music and any other questions the participants might raise. Teachers and family members would be encouraged to observe. Brochures describing BW's music degree programs would be available for distribution.

The Conservatory's highly competent Coordinator of Admissions, Mrs. Dorothy Wood, took charge of mailing announcements concerning the workshop and keeping track of responses, but as department head, I had to oversee the entire operation, from drafting the cover letter that was sent to potential applicants, to making sure the pianos were freshly tuned, to gearing myself up to serve as moderator for the afternoon discussion period. The latter job I likened to being a TV game show host. I could do only so much preparation; beyond that, I simply had to wing it.

Only about ten students attended the first year (1983), but all seemed pleased with the workshop agenda. At the afternoon session, one of the teachers made an impromptu speech, praising the BW Piano Department for sponsoring such a helpful and inspiring event.

The workshop became a highly effective recruiting tool for the department and was still going strong when I retired from BW in 1999. We made only minor changes through the years because our original format—the result of long weeks of spirited, sometimes contentious exchanges—worked. As my Daddy would have said, "If it ain't broke, don't fix it!"

While my heavy, relentless schedule began to take its toll on my body, my spirit remained strong. Although physically tired, I felt internally energized. For the first time in my life, I saw my professional potential being realized. Since my colleagues consistently complimented me on my efforts, I pressed on. Electing not to take advantage of my eligibility for a sabbatical leave in the fall of 1983, I decided instead to wait until the end of my term as department head.

With the wisdom of hindsight, I can now see clearly that I should have taken my sabbatical on schedule. I failed to recognize that my physically abnormal body was under extraordinary stress. A rest would have revitalized my physical strength and, perhaps, would have averted the health crisis that loomed on the horizon. I think my lapse of judgment is understandable, since I had spent my entire life more or less ignoring my limitations; but if I could, I would go back to that moment and change my decision.

I compounded my mistake by scheduling two performances of my new Mozart/Chopin program: first, in Bennettsville on August 22, under the auspices of the Marlboro Arts Council, and scarcely a month later at Baldwin Wallace on September 24.

These recitals proved to be among the most satisfying of my career. For the first time, without the supervision of a teacher, I had selected the repertoire and made every minute interpretive decision concerning tempo, phrasing, dynamic contrasts, rubato, voicing, and pedaling. Consequently, I felt that this music was, in a very real sense, "all mine," as if, more than ever before, I were sharing a part of my musical identity with the audience.

I HAD NOT PERFORMED IN BENNETTSVILLE since the 1970s, when I'd been a lowly graduate student. Now, as a tenured professor with a doctorate, I had to live up to my credentials.

The local newspaper, the *Marlboro Herald-Advocate,* offered spectacular coverage, presenting several preliminary articles, culminating in the August 18 issue with a front-page picture of me practicing in the auditorium and a headline that read, "VICKIE COVINGTON IN CONCERT AT 8:00 MONDAY NIGHT." The reporter wrote a detailed account of how I had overcome my physical limitations at the keyboard and exclaimed in a monumental understatement, "Dr. Covington and her music career have come a long way."

August 22, 1983: at the post-recital reception, with Faye Griggs Bell (left) and Fay McLaurin. Notice the braces on my teeth.

On August 22, friends and supporters filled the hall to capacity. Attending from out of town were two of my former college classmates with their children, as well as Dr. and Mrs. Horn and others from St. Andrews. My first two piano teachers, Faye Griggs Bell and Fay McLaurin, both said they had never heard me play better; Mother agreed. This unanimous verdict from my three staunchest supporters and toughest critics was a triumph.

Only the hot, muggy weather and the inadequacy of the hall's air-conditioning system marred the event. Playing the Mozart Sonata, the easiest piece on the program, left me dripping with sweat. From then on, every time I left the stage, I wheeled my chair over to a vent behind the curtain and parked for a moment, letting the cool air blow under my dress. Exhausted and dehydrated by the conclusion of the performance, I could hardly get out of bed the next day. I looked forward to September 24, when temperatures in Northern Ohio would be cool and comfortable.

My success in Bennettsville paved the way for me to play with unparalleled security and conviction at Baldwin Wallace. The response of colleagues, students, and friends had never been more positive. One of my best and favorite former students sent me this rave review:

Dear Dr. Covington,

Without a doubt, you are the most professional and musical pianist in the Conservatory.

I admire your Mozart especially and the concentrated, yet "relaxed" approach you bring to your performing. Bravo!

These bold words hit home. Obviously, my student regarded me not as a disabled pianist who had somehow overcome her limitations, but simply as a mature performer who had communicated effectively the aesthetic content of the music. My able-bodied colleagues, of course, could play louder and faster than I. Technically, I would never be their equal. However, in the areas of professionalism and musicality, my student implied that I was not only their equal, but their superior. I couldn't have felt more gratified.

MY RELAXED AND RESTFUL CHRISTMAS BREAK of 1983 ended ominously. On my last night in South Carolina, a red itching-burning bump appeared on my back; I disregarded it. After my arrival in Ohio, more itching-burning bumps appeared. I had never seen or felt anything like this. Ray took me to a doctor, who diagnosed me with shingles. I had a very mild case, lasting only a couple of weeks, but any case of shingles causes misery. I did not realize that the shingles were a symptom of my body's malfunctioning immune system.

Shortly after the shingles subsided, I got a throat infection and totally lost my voice. Mother flew to Cleveland in mid-January to stay with me for three or four days until I could return to my teaching. An antibiotic eliminated the infection, but I never regained my strength. In fact, I became increasingly weaker and thinner. One of my adult students, who had returned to college after many years as wife and mother, made a not-so-subtle reference to my weight loss: "Dr. Covington, do you know what your trouble is? You have no blubber for emergencies."

I received a letter on February 15, saying that the college's Promotion and Tenure Committee had unanimously recommended my promotion to the rank of associate professor, but I felt too sick to celebrate. Maintaining my schedule had become an uphill struggle. I awoke most mornings with terrible pains throughout my body. I began having a low-grade fever almost daily.

About a month before the end of the 1983-84 school year, I called Conservatory Director Warren Scharf, who had been aware of my declining health, and told him I had no choice but to take a medical leave of absence. He readily granted my request.

When I told my piano department colleagues, George Cherry volunteered right away to take over as department head and expressed confidence that his wife would be willing to assume my teaching duties. Everyone agreed that restoration of my well-being had to be my top priority.

In mid-May, I flew to South Carolina. Mother had already set up an appointment for me to see our family doctor. Following an examination and a battery of tests, he gave me his preliminary diagnosis—rheumatoid arthritis. He wanted his opinion corroborated by a specialist, so he sent me to Dr. John Rice, a rheumatologist at Duke University Medical Center in Durham, North Carolina.

Dr. Rice agreed with the diagnosis but ordered more tests. I was admitted to the hospital at Duke. I weighed eighty-eight pounds.

FACULTY RECITAL AT BALDWIN-WALLACE COLLEGE

Kulas Musical Arts Building
Berea, Ohio
October 8, 1977

Five Little Two-Voice Studies for Piano (1955) .... Lucia Alcalay
    Andante
    Allegro
    Lento
    Improvisando
    Vivace

Sonata in B-flat Major, K. 570 .... Mozart
    Allegro
    Adagio
    Allegretto

INTERMISSION

Four Mazurkas .... Chopin
    G Major, Op. 50, No. 1
    C Major, Op. 24, No. 2
    A Minor, Op. 67, No. 4
    B-flat Minor, Op. 24, No. 4

Nocturne in C-sharp Minor, Op. 27, No. 1 .... Chopin

Poems of the Sea .... Bloch
    Waves
    Chanty
    At Sea

Encore: "In Evening Air" .... A. Copland

CHAMBER MUSIC RECITAL
AT BALDWIN-WALLACE COLLEGE
WITH PAUL STATSKY, VIOLINIST

Kulas Musical Arts Building
Berea, Ohio
April 7, 1979

Sonata in E Minor, Op. 5, No. 8 .... Corelli
    Preludio
    Allemanda
    Sarabanda
    Giga

Sonata in E Minor, K. 304 .... Mozart
    Allegro
    Tempo di menuetto

Three Romances, Op. 94 .... Schumann

Sonatina in D Major, D. 384 .... Schubert
    Allegro molto
    Andante
    Allegro vivace

Note: We played this program in Bennettsville, S.C., in August 1979.

FACULTY RECITAL AT BALDWIN-WALLACE COLLEGE

Kulas Musical Arts Building
Berea, Ohio
April 3, 1982

Eight Piano Pieces (1946) .... Krenek
1. Etude   5. Nocturne
2. Invention   6. Waltz
3. Scherzo   7. Air
4. Toccata   8. Rondo

Sonata No. 38 in F Major (Hob. XVI: 23) .... Haydn
Moderato
Adagio
Finale – Presto

Five Mazurkas .... Chopin
B-flat Major, Op. 17, No. 1
F Minor, Op. 65, No. 2
G Minor, Op. 24, No. 1
A Minor, Op. 17, No. 4
A-flat Major, Op. 54, No. 2

Two Nocturne .... Chopin
F Minor, Op. 55, No. 1
C-sharp Minor, Op. 27, No. 1

FACULTY RECITAL AT BALDWIN-WALLACE COLLEGE

Kulas Musical Arts Building
Berea, Ohio
September 24, 1983

Sonata in C Major, K. 279 .... Mozart
  Allegro
  Andante
  Allegro

Adagio in B Minor, K. 540 .... Mozart

Two Nocturnes .... Chopin
  C-sharp Minor, Lento con gran espressione
  E-flat Major, Op. 55, No. 2

Four Mazurkas .... Chopin
  G Major, Op. 67, No. 1
  F Minor, Op. 7, No. 3
  E Minor, Op. 17, No. 2
  C-sharp Minor, Op. 50, No. 3

Encore: Nocturne in E-flat Major, Op. 9, No. 2 .... Chopin

*Note: I played this program in Bennettsville, S.C., on August
22, 1983, under the auspices of the Marlboro Arts Council.*

RHEUMATOID ARTHRITIS:
A GAME-CHANGER

MY CONGENITAL DISABILITY had been stable and painless, a mere "inconvenience." Rheumatoid arthritis (RA) abruptly changed the rules of the game. For the first time, I faced a chronic, progressive illness that allowed me to take nothing for granted, least of all my ability to play the piano. I knew that hands and wrists tend to be particularly vulnerable to the ravages of RA. I saw the crestfallen look on the faces of the occupational therapists (OTs) at Duke when I told them I was a pianist.

Trying to put the best face on a bad situation, Dr. Rice and my OTs emphasized that RA tends to progress slowly over a long period of time. True, I might eventually lose my pianistic career to RA, but by making wise choices, I could, with a little luck, push that eventuality far into the future. And there was always the possibility of remission.

Armed with this information, I decided instantly to do everything in my power to maintain my career as long as possible. After all I had been through to establish myself professionally, I was not about to give up without a fight. Dr. Rice remarked that my positive attitude, plus the thirty-eight years I had spent adjusting to my congenital disability, might actually give me an advantage in coping with RA. I saw his point, although I hardly considered it "advantageous" to be facing two disabling conditions.

Thus began the tedious, time-consuming task of reclaiming my life. Dr. Rice prepared me for a period of experimentation, as we determined which medications and dosages would be most effective for me. The OTs explained the intricacies of joint protection, a concept that must now govern every aspect of my daily routine. My first OT gave me this vivid illustration: "On any given day, you can expect only a limited amount of mileage from an arthritic hand. You have to decide how to spend that limited mileage. Do you really want to use arthritic hands to pull wet sheets out of a washer?" I vowed on the spot never again to do my own laundry and cleaning—and I never did.

As my pain levels gradually decreased, I made tentative plans to return to my Ohio apartment in the fall and perhaps resume teaching winter quarter. Lynne Cherry agreed to continue teaching for me until January. George graciously offered to serve the remainder of my term as department head.

As I prepared to make the transition back to the real world, the OTs gave me a wealth of common-sense suggestions for minimizing stress on my hands. In the bathroom, squeeze the toothpaste tube with my forearm instead of my fingers. In the kitchen, switch to lightweight dishes and plastic utensils, drink from a straw to avoid lifting a glass, and divide large quantities of food into smaller containers. In dressing myself, avoid styles that are difficult to put on and take off and replace buttons with Velcro. Most important, I purchased a motorized chair to use whenever I left my apartment alone. The OTs had warned me that pushing myself manually down the long, heavily carpeted hallways at Tower in the Park would be disastrous for my hands.

IN JANUARY 1985, my life seemed to be getting back to normal. I returned to teaching, and my orthodontist removed my braces. I celebrated the latter milestone by polishing off a large jar of chunky peanut butter.

Unfortunately, by early spring, my right hand and wrist showed unmistakable signs of arthritic damage. If I played the piano for more than ten or fifteen minutes, I felt intense, burning pain across the top of my hand. Seemingly overnight, my wrist "dropped." I could not raise it to a normal position. The thumb joint nearest the nail completely collapsed. I could actually move the squishy flesh from side to side, and if I happened to bump it sideways, I'd gasp and see stars.

Agreeing with me that surgical intervention was imperative, Dr. Rice arranged a consultation with Dr. James Urbaniak, Duke's top hand surgeon (and one of the best in the country), shortly after my arrival in South Carolina for the summer. Dr. Urbaniak said he had never seen a hand exactly like mine—hardly a reassuring comment, but I appreciated his candor. In July, he performed extensive surgery, raising my right wrist to a more normal position, widening the space between my thumb and index finger (to give me more "reach" at the keyboard), and fusing the collapsed joint in my right thumb. At the start of fall quarter, I still wore a splint and had no idea what the ultimate outcome would be.

RAY KUBACKI'S IMPENDING DEPARTURE from Tower in the Park added to my turmoil; he and his ex-wife planned to remarry. My relationship with Ray had taken a romantic turn about six months after we met, although neither of us sought a permanent commitment. I still clung tenaciously to my independence, and he nourished the hope of someday reclaiming his marriage. Now that his hope was about to be realized, I found myself torn between happiness for him and his family and despair at the prospect of losing the man who had been both a devoted friend and a lifeline of assistance for the past seven years. Setting aside emotional issues, I zeroed in on the urgent practicality of finding someone to escort me to and from my car on teaching days.

An elderly friend recommended a young woman named Irene ("Renie") Martin, who lived in the building with her husband and three-year-old son. Renie's evening job at a local community college meant that she would likely be free to help me during the day. We worked out an arrangement whereby, for a modest wage, she would come to my apartment in the morning, take me to my car, put my chair in its backseat spot, and send me on my way to BW. In the afternoon they would meet me at the carport, push me back to my apartment, and get me settled. Renie and I bonded almost instantly, and I fell in love with handsome little Jimmy.

My morale received a further boost when my sister Mary Jo called to say that her job as assistant manager with Designer Depot (a subsidiary of Kmart) would soon bring her to Stow, Ohio, only an hour's drive from Berea. Shortly thereafter, she and her new husband, Jack Harris, moved even closer to me, when she was transferred to a store in Willoughby Hills on the east side of Cleveland. During the next three years, our outings and excursions provided me with much-needed R and R. For the first time since our youth, Mary Jo and I saw each other regularly, and thanks to Jack's stellar culinary talents, I managed to gain a few pounds.

I ACCOMPANIED MOTHER to a tennis tournament in Lexington, Kentucky, in July 1986. She had promised that between matches, we'd tour the surrounding area—my first chance to see thoroughbred racehorses up close. An employee at our hotel mapped out an itinerary that took us through spectacular countryside and several horse farms. At Kentucky Horse Park, I saw "Forego," still looking strong and magnificent in retirement.

MY SABBATICAL LEAVE of fall quarter 1986 and winter quarter 1987 gave me the opportunity to rebuild my keyboard technique. Initially, I felt discouraged. Although the surgery had relieved my pain, it had not restored my right hand to its pre-arthritis strength and agility. Moreover, Dr. Urbaniak and two OTs confirmed that the new limitations were permanent. With my performing career still very much in doubt, I began—cautiously and carefully—a regular, yet flexible, practice regimen. By November, I had put together a short program consisting of eight Schubert waltzes and two Chopin nocturnes, including my favorite, in C-sharp minor.

Next I had to test myself by presenting informal performances for small, sympathetic audiences. The first of these took place on November 24 in my apartment, so that I'd have the security of playing my own piano. Ruth and Don Pickering took charge of inviting the guests, providing refreshments, and bringing in extra chairs. Mary Jo and Jack attended, along with about eight friends from Tower in the Park. After my arrival in South Carolina for the Christmas holidays, I played the same program for a church group and at a home for senior citizens. The success of these festive events renewed my faith in miracles; I felt no less satisfaction than when I had played in major concert halls.

I had learned, however, that as an arthritic pianist, I would have to be more selective than ever in choosing repertoire for performance and more innovative than ever in solving technical problems at the keyboard. Although Dr. Urbaniak was essentially correct in saying that there would be no improvement in the function of my right hand, I did observe an increase in my overall strength and stamina, which benefited my playing immensely.

DUSTING OFF MY LITERARY SKILLS, I wrote three articles during my sabbatical. "Operatic Elements in the Music of

Chopin," a condensation of my master's thesis, appeared in the September 1987 issue of *The American Music Teacher*, the same journal that had presented Martha Mehta's "A Job For Emily" fourteen years earlier. A brief autobiographical essay, "Conserves Energy to Make Music," was published in the Fall 1990 issue of *Accent on Living*, a magazine devoted to the needs and issues of the physically disabled. Having read several articles in *Piano Quarterly* about the physical problems of pianists, I made a spur-of-the-moment decision to send a letter to the editor, summarizing my background and experience. To my surprise, the very next issue contained my letter. To my even greater surprise, I heard from a woman in California, who wrote, "Dear Victoria: After reading your letter, I have decided not to give up playing the piano." As I read these words, a shiver ran through my whole body. Obviously, I had bolstered the morale of a total stranger. Perhaps, I thought, I should seek more opportunities to tell my story.

I relished my return to the college in March. My sabbatical had been productive and enjoyable; moreover, in my absence the Conservatory building had undergone much-needed, long-anticipated renovations. Waiting for me would be a shiny, new, state-of-the-art elevator.

WHEN RENIE AND HER FAMILY moved into a house in a nearby community, our friendship remained strong, but I needed someone in the building to help me to and from my car on teaching days. I found the ideal candidate in Mrs. Lucille ("Lue") Fletcher, a widow in her early seventies who had plenty of time on her hands and was looking for a way to earn some extra money. Lue's adoration of her three grown sons did not preclude her adopting me as the daughter she never had. Lue anchored my support system for eight years until she fell and broke her right wrist. Even then, she wanted to continue, but I told her in no uncertain terms that she should consider herself retired.

THE 1987-88 ACADEMIC YEAR can only be described as a year of fireworks, beginning with my comeback faculty recital on Sunday afternoon, September 20. Students, faculty, and friends enthusiastically welcomed my return to public performance. Mary Jo and Jack hosted a splendid post-recital reception in the party room at Tower in the Park. The menu featured some of Jack's most mouthwatering goodies. I still recall vividly the exhilaration I felt going from table to table greeting well-wishers.

I found the following note from my colleague, George Cherry, in my mailbox at the Conservatory on Monday morning:

Dear Vickie,

What a treat to hear you again! Your preparation was, as always, thoroughness itself.

But though the musical presentation was first-rate, I was especially pleased for you, knowing what a personal satisfaction it must have been to triumph over the odds!

I hope you're basking in the glory today—and for some time to come.

Love,

George

Scarcely a month after the recital, I received the University of Illinois Rehabilitation Division's highest accolade, the Harold Scharper Achievement Award, which had been established in 1950 to honor Harold Scharper, the first paraplegic to attend UIUC. During my student years, I had seen the plaque prominently displayed at the rehab center, bearing the names of each year's winner. I never dreamed that one day I would be in this illustrious company.

September 20, 1987: Mary Jo took this picture shortly before the performance.

Mary Jo and Jack drove me from Cleveland to Champaign for the awards banquet on October 17; Mother and Daddy made the trip from South Carolina. What a proud and humbling moment to be recognized by one of the country's most outstanding rehabilitation programs and to be personally congratulated by Mr. Konitzki and Professor Tim Nugent (Founder and Director Emeritus of the UIUC Rehabilitation Center).

Shortly after the *Marlboro Herald-Advocate* printed a story about my Scharper Award, a letter arrived informing me that the Bennettsville Rotary Club had voted me Non-Resident Handicapped Citizen of the Year. Mother and Daddy attended the dinner and accepted this honor on my behalf. Mother told me later that she had thanked the group for "loving Vickie as

148

much as we do." Fay McLaurin's husband, Colin, a paraplegic since World War II, received the Resident award. The next time I saw him, we heartily congratulated each other.

The grand finale, yet to come, requires a bit of background information.

When Mr. Konitzki called to say that he and Dr. Joseph Larsen (director of the rehab center) wanted to nominate me for the bronze Medallion of Honor, I had no idea what he meant. He explained that the UIUC Mothers' Association created the award in 1966 to pay tribute to individuals who, by example and service, had used their talents to enrich the lives of others. The first recipient was actress Helen Hayes. Senator Margaret Chase Smith received the Medallion in 1968. Since 1977, the award has been given annually to a woman affiliated in some way with the University of Illinois. Mr. Konitzki said, to his knowledge, no one with a physical disability had ever received the medallion; he and Dr. Larsen wanted me to be the first. Agreeing to the nomination seemed like reaching for the moon, and frankly, the thought of another award seemed like overkill. However, I could hardly decline their kind and generous gesture, so I agreed.

I needed an additional recommendation, and Mr. Konitzki suggested that I ask a UIUC musician. Dean Sanders seemed the perfect choice. When I called him, he exclaimed ecstatically: "Vickie! This is a huge deal. Of course, I'll support your nomination. By the way, did you know that the woman who designed the moon buggy, the vehicle used by the astronauts to explore the surface of the moon, is a medallion recipient?" Talk about reaching for the moon! Dean also told me that he was personally acquainted with Mary Burch, who had presented the first medallion to Helen Hayes. "If you're the winner, I'll invite Mary to be my guest at the awards banquet," he said. I felt myself getting caught up in the excitement, but I made a valiant effort to put the matter out of my mind and carry on with my usual routine.

Answering the phone one evening in early March, I had no inkling that I would hear an extremely cordial woman say, "Dr. Covington, I'm calling on behalf of the University of Illinois Mothers'Association to congratulate you on being chosen as this year's Medallion of Honor recipient." Had I not been sitting in my wheelchair, I'm quite sure I would have collapsed onto the floor.

A follow-up letter from the association outlined the events that I would be attending during Moms'Weekend, April 22-23. A flurry of preparation ensued. Mary Jo arranged a day off from work, so she and Jack could drive me to and from Champaign. Mary Jo also took me shopping for new clothes: "If you're going to get this award, you have to look the part," she said. Mother and Daddy made plans for the long trek from South Carolina.

The occasion exceeded my highest expectations. Three rooms had been reserved for us at the Illini Union in the heart of the UIUC campus. My room, newly renovated for physical accessibility, contained every imaginable convenience, including a phone next to the toilet.

I received the medallion during the Mothers' Association banquet Friday evening with about 500 parents and students in attendance, as well as my family and my sponsors, Joe Konitzki, Joe Larsen, and Dean Sanders. The latter did indeed bring Mary Burch. I had mentally prepared my acceptance speech, but I never wrote a word of it.

The medallion, designed by David Wickersheimer, an architecture student in the UIUC College of Fine and Applied Arts, is a beautiful disc of solid bronze, eleven inches in circumference. The obverse symbolizes the service activities of the Mothers'Association, which encompass the University of Illinois and the enlightenment resulting from the university's achievements. The lettering and the Assembly Hall (a UIUC landmark) are combined to suggest a lamp of learning, shaped like the letter "G." On the reverse side, the design signifies the bestowal of honor upon an individual who, by example and service, brings enrichment into the lives of others. Abstract hands symbolize the giving of one's talents. The words *service* and *honor* appear across the top with my name engraved at the bottom. The medallion was presented to me in a handsome wooden base along with a bouquet of red roses. (The roses had been sent by two of Mother's tennis friends.)

As I entered the Illini Union Ballroom for the coffee hour on Saturday morning, a Dixieland band, made up of retired music professors, called the Medicare Five was performing. The trombonist of the group, Morris Carter, had been Assistant Director of the School of Music when I entered UIUC in 1968. Our friendship had begun when he—a native Kentuckian—first noticed my Southern accent.

When Mr. Carter saw me enter the ballroom, he took the microphone and announced: "Folks, this year's Medallion of Honor winner, Vickie Covington, has just joined us. She and I have been friends for many years. The Medicare Five would like to do a special song for her. Perhaps you've heard the old standard, *If You Knew Susie Like I Know Susie*. Well, we're going to change the lyrics a bit and dedicate this to Vickie." The vocalist stepped forward, and the ensemble launched into a spirited rendition of "If You Knew Vickie Like I Know Vickie . . . Oh, Oh, Oh, what a girl!" Touched, thrilled, and thoroughly delighted, I felt nothing short of total euphoria. As the song unfolded, my mind flashed back through my Illinois years—the hardships, the disappointments, the friendships, the accomplishments—all of which seemed to culminate in the present moment. Never in a million years would I have pictured myself in that ballroom, being serenaded by Morris Carter and his band.

Daddy, who had come into the ballroom during the performance, approached me, grinning broadly: "Do you know the expression, 'walking in high cotton'"?

Being a farmer's daughter, I said, "Of course." We smiled. Nothing more needed to be said.

THE MEDALLION OF HONOR TEA—the *pièce de résistance*—took place Saturday afternoon at the home of the president of the university. When I first learned that one hundred invitations to the tea had already been printed, I panicked. I had not lived in Champaign-Urbana fulltime since 1975; many of the people I knew and worked with had moved away. With Nancy Stagg's help, I compiled a list of about forty professors, friends, classmates, and acquaintances who were still in the area. The remaining invitations were sent to friends and relatives across the country, even though I knew these people could not attend.

As we made our way to the elegant mansion, I couldn't help thinking of that day in the fall of 1968 when Mother and Daddy had left me at the rehab center to return to South Carolina, all three of us scared to death and literally in tears. If someone had told us that almost twenty years later, we'd be going to the president's home for a party in my honor, we would have seriously questioned their sanity.

No one awaited the party more eagerly than my dear friend, Barbara Ann Bauer. She had been completing her Ph.D. in English, when I met her during my final year as residence hall advisor. Barb's cerebral palsy makes walking hazardous, speaking difficult, and driving a car impossible, so I recruited Mother and Daddy to provide her transportation.

I had Barb's street address and apartment number but did not know the exact location. "Don't worry," Mother assured me cheerily. "We'll just keep asking for directions until we find her."

152

Away they went, returning with Barb in a relatively short time. She hugged me long and hard, and then sat next to me throughout the "calling hours," so that we could chat whenever I wasn't greeting other guests.

I think virtually everyone on the invitation list attended. How happy I felt, reconnecting with people I had not seen in seven or more years. I was especially glad to be able to express my gratitude to some of my most significant professors, whose guidance and support had facilitated my professional success.

I'd wondered whether Dr. Leonhard would make an appearance. I had it on good authority that his idea of a party was beer and poker with the guys. He not only came; he even wore a suit and tie. I had never seen him so elegantly attired. I greeted him enthusiastically and thanked him profusely for his presence. "You know, I don't often go to *teas,*" he growled, but he smiled and gave me a big kiss. "As a matter of fact, I can't think of anyone else's tea I'd go to." I have seldom felt more amused or more flattered.

By 4:00 p.m., I was bidding a fond, grateful farewell to my Mothers' Association hosts, who had made my Medallion of Honor experience an extravaganza in the best sense of the word. Since the drive back to Cleveland took eight hours, and the drive to Bennettsville much longer, we all decided to leave Champaign right away, rather than spend another night on campus.

Come Monday morning, my life would return to normal, but I knew I would be giddy with leftover excitement for a long time. Daddy made an *á propos* comment as we departed: "Vickie, I've heard of being queen for a day, but you were queen for a whole weekend."

MY DECISION in the spring of 1988 to sell my car and hire a driver brought intense relief to all who had followed with fear and trembling my escapades behind the wheel. Don Pickering spoke for everyone: "Vickie, you have no idea how much better I'll sleep at night, knowing you're not out there on the road."

Driving, which had never been easy for me, had become even more difficult and stressful as my arthritis worsened, and if I continued to drive, I faced the prospect of buying a new car. The Fury bore the scars of twelve Cleveland winters; to make matters worse, I had also managed to bang the driver's side door into the wall of my carport on three separate occasions. What can I say? Sharp left turns were not my forté. The third time, I had sheared off the door handle, but I didn't bother to have it fixed, since I got in and out from the passenger side.

Mary Jo and Jack pointed out that hiring a driver would save me money in the long run, given the cost of a new car, not to mention other essentials, like insurance, maintenance, gas, and carport. I agreed—but in order to hire a driver, I first had to find one.

Negotiations with a couple of local cab companies proved futile. However, while I was in South Carolina for spring break, Jack struck pay dirt when he saw an ad in Cleveland's newspaper, *The Plain Dealer*. The woman placing the ad would provide transportation for grocery shopping, medical appointments, and other errands. Jack called the woman and explained my situation. She promised to talk with me before committing herself to anyone else.

Geraldine ("Gerri") Jeris told me that after going through a recent divorce, she needed to supplement her income. My four-day-a-week teaching schedule appealed to her, and her proximity to Tower in the Park (twenty minutes away) meant that she'd be spending only about an hour each day taking me to and from the college. We agreed to a trial period of two weeks at seven dollars a trip.

Gerri served as my regular driver for the next three years and remained my dear friend until her fatal bout with cancer. She and I could hardly have been more different, but there was a spark of mutual affection and respect between us that solidified our relationship from the moment we met. Before long, she had reduced my fare to six dollars a trip.

I loved Gerri's exuberance and spontaneity. She'd call me on one of my days off: "Vickie! When was the last time you did something just for fun?" If I paused before responding, she'd interject, "Just as I thought. Let's go to a movie!"

Gerri seemed the antithesis of the classical music buff, yet she was the first person to take me to Severance Hall to hear the Cleveland Orchestra. We went to two or three concerts each season. After a couple of years, she finally let me pay for my ticket.

She made no attempt to hide her only vice: gambling. One Monday morning, she picked me up, looking more frazzled than usual. "Oh, m'gosh," she sputtered. "I thought I'd be late. Thirty minutes ago, I was pushing my way through a crowded plane." She had flown to Atlantic City for the weekend.

Gerri introduced me to her brother Jim, who soon became a loyal friend, taking over as my driver when needed. After my retirement, the three of us continued to get together periodically for lunch at the Olive Garden. "Today is Jim's treat," Gerri would invariably say. Jim never disagreed.

MARY JO WAS TEMPORARILY AT LOOSE ENDS when she learned that Kmart would soon close all of its Designer Depot stores; I was temporarily at loose ends when I learned that her new position as assistant manager with Marshall's would require her to move to Greenville, South Carolina, to open a store there. She and Jack headed south in early summer 1988. They hated leaving me as much as I hated seeing them go. On the other hand, Jack luxuriated in their return to a warmer climate. Having grown up in Florida, my big tough brother-in-law couldn't take the Cleveland winters, and of course, Mary Jo welcomed the opportunity to be closer to Mother and Daddy.

MY RECITAL IN BENNETTSVILLE on July 11, 1988, billed as "Music for a Summer's Evening," featured the same repertoire I had played at BW the previous September. Fay McLaurin had devised the fanciful rubric.

Media hype included extensive coverage in the *Marlboro Herald-Advocate* and a lengthy radio interview, which aired frequently in the days leading up to the performance. I feared that too much information might actually turn people off and make them less likely to come hear me.

My worry proved needless, as appreciative listeners packed the hall. The young man who had recently purchased and renovated Gran's house surprised me by hiring a professional photographer, who not only took pictures, but also videotaped the program. My playing that night, although not my absolute best, satisfied my toughest critics—Faye Griggs Bell, Fay McLaurin, and Mother.

"ON TECHNIQUE AND CREATIVITY IN MUSIC: Conversation with Victoria Covington" appeared in the summer/fall 1989 issue of *Kaleidoscope*, an international magazine devoted to "exploring the experience of disability through literature and the fine arts" (www.KaleidoscopeOnline.org, Kaleidoscope@udsakron.org). Gail Willmott, a close friend of mine since my Allen Hall days at UIUC, had joined *Kaleidoscope's* editorial staff in '82. (She is now editor-in-chief.) It was her idea to include an article about my musical career in this particular volume, which focused on disability and the performing arts.

When I received Gail's list of probing questions, I groaned;

156

however, formulating the answers proved both rewarding and cathartic. I had reached a crossroads. It remained unclear how rheumatoid arthritis would alter the quality and longevity of my professional life. Nevertheless, I found myself responding confidently when asked, "What are the essential qualities that have allowed you to continue adapting and looking forward?"

Throughout my life my family, teachers, colleagues, and friends have encouraged me to develop all of my abilities to the fullest extent possible. With their support I have, for the most part, maintained a realistic, matter-of-fact attitude toward my disability so that, quite frankly, I have never thought seriously about not continuing to adapt and look forward. There have always been so many things I could do that it seemed stupid to sit around worrying about the things I couldn't do. Music has provided an ideal focus for my enthusiasm and energy, and I believe that this sense of purpose has allowed me to solve problems—or at least cope with them— more easily.

By the spring of 1989, as my RA gradually worsened (no sign of remission), teaching consumed all my energy. Pacing myself had become a delicate balancing act, in which the slightest misstep could trigger an arthritic flare-up. Fortunately, BW readily granted my request for a halftime teaching load, beginning in September. I knew I could live comfortably on a reduced salary, and the college generously allowed me to keep my tenured rank and benefits. While I remained optimistic about the future, sensing that many satisfying and memorable experiences lay ahead, I also heard the inevitable ticking of the clock, telling me that despite my best efforts, the pianistic chapter of my life would end prematurely.

CONSERVES ENERGY TO MAKE MUSIC
(Published in the fall 1990 issue of *Accent On Living* magazine)

Had I written this article several years ago, it would have been essentially a story of "woman overcomes disability and achieves happy ending." At that time, I was beginning my eighth year as a member of the piano faculty at the Baldwin-Wallace Conservatory of Music. I was also serving my first term as head of the piano department. My doctorate in music education had been completed just two summers earlier. I had recently played two successful solo concerts.

What role had my physical disability played in all of this? It had been simply a fact of life, something that over the years I had learned to deal with almost subconsciously. When I was born, virtually all of my joints were "abnormal." When a series of orthopedic operations during my childhood failed to enable me to walk independently, I increasingly relied on a wheelchair.

True, my piano technique had always been unorthodox. I pedaled with my left foot. With my left hand, I frequently played notes intended for the right hand—and vice versa. My fingerings were untraditional to say the least. Because of my small right hand and abnormal wrist, I could not perform pieces with large reaches and big chords. In short, my disability had been primarily an "inconvenience." I had no pain and my health was excellent.

My situation changed drastically with the onset of rheumatoid arthritis during 1984. I had to take a leave of absence from my teaching. Pain became a part of daily life. Within a year of the diagnosis, my right thumb had completely collapsed and had withdrawn underneath my hand, and my right hand was pointing down at almost a 90-degree angle. I could scarcely reach a sixth at the keyboard—and after playing only a few minutes, I had persistent, burning pain across the back of my hand.

During the summer of 1985, one of the country's top hand surgeons operated on my right wrist and fused my right thumb.

I have returned to my teaching position at Baldwin-Wallace, and I am playing the piano again—somewhat awkwardly, but without pain. The surgery restored about 50 percent of my previous piano facility in my right hand.

Living with a chronic, progressive illness is very different from living with a stable condition that is merely inconvenient. I have new perceptions of myself and what is normal for me. The hard reality is that if I want to continue playing the piano, I must save my hands for that purpose. Consequently, I no longer do my own laundry and houschold cleaning. I use a motorized chair for long distances. I type my correspondence on an electric typewriter.

My sense of well-being has gradually returned; anger and frustration have diminished; my level of pain has decreased; and my energy level has improved. I have a renewed appreciation of skills I formerly took for granted; of family and friends, on whose help and support I must increasingly depend; and of my own fortitude.

LETTER TO THE EDITOR OF
THE PIANO QUARTERLY
(Published in the spring1987 issue)

To the editor:

I have been very gratified to see the concern shown by *The Piano Quarterly* for pianists whose professional lives and livelihoods have been threatened by physical problems. It is a subject close to my heart and personal experience! I have been a performing pianist since the age of eight—and physically disabled from birth.

Fortunately for my pianistic career, the worst of my congenitally malformed joints were my right leg and hip. Although I rely on a wheelchair for mobility, I am able to stand and transfer to the piano bench when playing. My left leg is quite strong enough for the damper pedal. My left hand has always been relatively strong and virtually normal. My right hand and wrist are smaller, weaker, and more limited in flexibility.

Of course, my piano technique has always been unorthodox. With my left hand, I frequently play notes intended for the right hand, and *vice versa*. My fingerings are sometimes untraditional to say the least. I must select carefully the repertoire that I perform, avoiding pieces with large reaches and thick chords. However, within the scope of repertoire that I *can* play, I have had the satisfaction of knowing that my performances are technically and musically convincing.

For the first thirty-seven years of my life, my disability was a stable condition, which I simply accepted and eventually learned to cope with almost instinctively. It did not interfere with my musical education, including master's and doctoral degrees from the University of Illinois; it did not preclude my being asked to join the piano faculty at the Baldwin Wallace Conservatory of Music.

Three years ago, however, an attack of rheumatoid arthritis brought about a drastically different set of circumstances. I found myself confronted with a chronic, progressive illness that allowed me to take nothing for granted, least of all my ability to play the piano. Arthritic damage to my right hand was particularly swift and devastating; surgery was necessary during the summer of 1985.

I have recently made a modest comeback as a performer, presenting short, informal programs for a gathering of friends and neighbors, a church group, and a retirement community. My success so far makes me cautiously optimistic that I will be able to present a program at Baldwin Wallace during the coming year, perhaps in a lecture-recital format.

I realize that in the future I will have to be more selective than ever in choosing repertoire for performance, more innovative than ever in solving technical problems, more patient and persevering than ever in allowing sufficient time for my body (and spirit) to adjust to constantly changing definitions of "normal."

Above all, I must keep intact my sense of musical integrity. If I am described as "no ordinary pianist," I want it to be not just because of my unusual physical circumstances, but because of the musical quality of my playing.

Victoria Covington
Associate Professor of Piano
Baldwin-Wallace College

FACULTY RECITAL AT BALDWIN-WALLACE COLLEGE

Kulas Musical Arts Building
Berea, Ohio
September 20, 1987

Sketches in Color .... Starer
    Purple
    Shades of Blue
    Black and White
    Bright Orange
    Grey
    Pink
    Crimson

Ten Waltzes and German Dances
    (selected from Opera 9a, 9b, 18, 33, and 50) .... Schubert

Nocturne in E Minor (No. 10, Peters Ed.) .... Field

Nocturne in F Major (No. 16, Peters Ed.)............................ Field

Nocturne in C-sharp Minor, Op. 27, No. 1 .... Chopin

Note: I played this program in Bennettsville, S.C., on July 11, 1988 ("Music for a Summer's Evening").

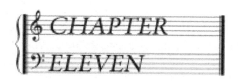

COMMON SENSE MIRACLES

DURING MY UNIVERSITY OF ILLINOIS YEARS, my rehab friends frequently attended my recitals. There they were—sitting in their wheelchairs, parked at the front of the hall, a row of smiling admirers. Lurking in the back of my mind was the threat, made by one or two mischievous members of the group, that when I stood to transfer to the piano bench, they would call out, "It's a miracle! It's miracle!" I countered with a threat of my own: "If you think you're disabled now, just wait . . . "

After I moved to Ohio, a woman approached me one day as I entered the lobby of Tower in the Park in my motorized chair. Taking my hand, she looked me straight in the eye and crooned, "Don't worry, dear. I'll pray for a miracle." I was speechless.

Later, I realized that I should have sat that woman down and said, "Let me tell you about miracles. Despite my congenital disability, I fulfilled my dream of becoming a teaching and performing pianist. I earned my master's and doctoral degrees at a major Midwestern university. I am now a member of the piano faculty at Baldwin Wallace. I am maintaining my career despite a second disabling condition, rheumatoid arthritis. Need I go on?"

I have never witnessed a cataclysmic miracle. On the other hand, I consider myself to be an expert in the "common sense" kind of miracle that is built minute-by-minute, day-by-day, one-decision-at-a-time. Based on this pragmatic definition, my final years at BW were nothing short of miraculous.

HALF-TIMETEACHING substantially reduced my levels of stress and fatigue. There were fewer arthritic flare-ups, and I actually had enough energy to live my life. Lynne Cherry, who had amply demonstrated her first-rate pedagogical skills, took the remainder of my load.

As a performer, I decided to learn a new recital program every two years and to schedule my performances very early in the fall, when I would be fresh from the summer's practicing and relatively unruffled by the pressures of teaching and other professional duties.

My strategies for pianistic success were extensions of the philosophy that had proved successful throughout my career. My number-one assumption: In order to play in a convincing manner, I had to be physically comfortable. As an arthritic, that meant, "If it hurts, don't do it." I had to assess my physical limitations accurately and use those limitations as boundaries in the selection of repertoire.

Before arthritis, I could play a sizable portion of the piano literature. Consequently, I could plan programs with relative ease. After arthritis, repertoire selection became a finely honed art. The progressive deterioration of my hands complicated the situation. With each performance, I had a new limitation to consider. Stamina became a constant concern. I found, to my great frustration, that frequently I had to set aside a piece I could play and wanted to play simply because practicing it proved excessively tiring.

On the positive side, my search for suitable repertoire led me to some delightful treasures. I discovered that numerous twentieth-century composers had written children's pieces that were artistic, subtle, and thoroughly appropriate for adult audiences. Returning to my romantic roots, I relearned some of Felix Mendelssohn's *Songs Without Words*, finding them just as expressively rewarding as when I had been introduced to them forty years earlier. I hit the jackpot when I read an article in one of my professional journals about Felix's older sister, Fanny Mendelssohn Hensel, whose compositions were just beginning to be published. The pieces proved to be quite lovely, and I could actually play several of them.

By scouring the literature, I put together four musically interesting, technically comfortable recitals, which I performed at BW in September of 1990, 1992, 1994, and 1996. I presented two of these in Bennettsville—in August of 1991 and March of 1995. Preparing these programs put my skills of adaptation and innovation to the supreme test. I had spent much of my life devising unorthodox technical solutions at the keyboard, but I now considered absolutely nothing off limits, as long as I preserved the musical integrity of the piece and enhanced the musicality of the performance. From time to time my colleagues asked exactly how I had executed a certain passage. Usually, I would divulge my secret. Occasionally, I'd just say, "You really don't want to know!"

The bottom line: I had to be a perfectionist, aspiring to the same sound that any musically expressive pianist would strive for, disabled or not. Determined that my physical problems, although necessarily seen by the audience, must never be heard, I had to coax musically perfect performances from increasingly imperfect hands.

Spoken commentary, prepared and memorized as thoroughly as the music (no "uh's" or "and-uh's" allowed), became an integral part of every performance in my post-arthritis years. My remarks were originally intended to benefit students and non-musicians in the audience, but soon, musicians and amateurs alike were telling me that they enjoyed the verbal aspect of my programs as much as the music. Presenting the life and works of Fanny

Mendelssohn Hensel was particularly gratifying. I found that a surprising number of people didn't even know Felix had an older sister.

ON A SUNDAY AFTERNOON in April 1993, my colleagues and I presented a recital to dedicate a new Steinway grand piano that had recently been donated to BW's chapel. I played only two pieces by Fanny Mendelssohn, but the occasion represented a crucial turning point for me because I instantly fell in love with the piano, which proved to be much easier to play than the instrument in the Conservatory's large auditorium. I further realized that in the chapel's intimate sanctuary my small-scale repertoire would be totally appropriate and my spoken commentary easily heard. In short, I knew this would be the ideal venue for my future performances at BW.

My first faculty recital in the chapel, entitled "Romantic Miniatures," took place on September 17, 1994. The program offered a satisfying blend of unity and variety. I opened with selections from *Enfantines* by Ernest Bloch, a twentieth-century composer whose works bear the unmistakable stamp of nineteenth-century Romanticism. The second segment, a potpourri of "parlor music" by mostly obscure composers, included Rohde's exuberant *Dance of the Dragonflies*, Kohler's humorous *Cock-a-Doodle Waltz*, and Sandré's poignant *Requiem for a Little Bird*.

Fay McLaurin and I had agreed that the program should conclude with pieces by legitimate, mainstream Romantic composers. One can't get any more legitimate and mainstream than Chopin, so I returned to a little F-minor etude that I had learned at UIUC—a seldom heard piece, saturated with rhythmic complexity and expressive subtlety, but relatively simple in terms of technical execution. I followed the etude with Chopin's gorgeous and justifiably famous *Prelude in A Major* and finished with my favorite *Boat-Song in A Major* from Felix Mendelssohn's *Songs Without Words*.

As I polished my spoken commentary and practiced going straight through the program, I sensed that this could be one of the most successful performances of my career—if I kept my nerves under control. While the intimacy of the chapel offered certain advantages, the disadvantage was that the audience, especially people sitting in the front row, would be very close to me. The physical and emotional distance afforded by a spacious stage and large hall would be totally absent.

Last-minute developments conspired against my attempts to remain calm and collected. First, I received a message from the Office of College Relations, informing me that Wilma Salisbury, music critic of *The Plain Dealer*, wanted to meet me at the chapel for an interview. I had heard of Wilma for years; now I would meet her in person! We had a pleasant chat, after which I played a couple of pieces for her. The article, "Pianist Concentrates on Playing, Not Disability," and a picture appeared on the front page of the cultural section along with an announcement giving the date, time, and location of the recital. This publicity created quite a buzz in the BW community.

Capping the excitement, Dady Mehta called to say that he and Martha planned to make the two-and-a-half-hour drive from Ann Arbor, Michigan, to attend the recital. As much as I wanted to see them, I was apprehensive. The Mehtas were well aware of my struggles with arthritis, but they had heard none of my recent performances. How would they react to the obvious decline in my technical facility at the keyboard? Dady had always specialized in playing the biggest, most profound works of piano literature. What would he think about my modest collection of miniatures? Going about my daily routine, I felt a bit like Paul

Revere as I found myself chanting, "The Mehtas are coming! The Mehtas are coming!" Dady understood perfectly my wish not to see him until after the performance. He and Martha readily accepted my invitation to attend the post-recital reception, hosted by Ruth Pickering in her apartment.

ON THE NIGHT OF SEPTEMBER 17, about 200 people filled the chapel to capacity. As my stage manager wheeled me to the piano, warm, enthusiastic applause greeted me; my nerves melted away. Glancing around the room, I began by saying, "I think everyone I know must be here." There was a twitter of laughter, and I promptly got down to business. When the last chord of the Mendelssohn *Boat Song* had subsided, I lifted my hands from the keyboard. The audience erupted, rising from their seats, virtually in unison—my first standing ovation at BW.

Everyone pronounced the program a stunning success, and I received rave reviews from the Mehtas, who seldom give rave reviews. Dady had nothing but praise for my spoken commentary: "I can play for audiences," he confessed, "but I could never talk to them the way you do."

I mailed a copy of the recital video to Dean Sanders, who sent me a marvelously reassuring letter, saying that ten years of arthritis had in no way damaged the essence of my playing and that I was still "one of the angels." On October 31, 1994, I answered:

> *I have read and reread your wonderful letter…If you say I'm still one of the angels, that's good enough for me!*
>
> *Thank you for saying that I played "lovingly." Someone here told me that she liked my playing because I wasn't afraid to wear my heart on my sleeve. As much as I've always loved to play, my performances in recent years*

have had special meaning. It seems like a miracle that I am able to play at all after the events of the past ten years; I want to prolong and share that miracle as long as possible. I take great strength from my friends and supporters—and you, my dear friend, are at the top of the list.

IN BENNETTSVILLE, Fay McLaurin's involvement with a project to convert the historic downtown movie theater into a civic center prompted her to suggest that I assist in their fundraising efforts by presenting my "Romantic Miniatures" as a benefit concert. I happily complied. The recital, sponsored by the Bennettsville Music Club, took place during my spring break on March 23, 1995. I played just as confidently as I had in Ohio. "You nailed it!" Fay exulted. "You absolutely nailed it!" The event raised about $1,000, which helped pay for handicapped access at the civic center.

LATER THAT SPRING, a Pennsylvania piano teacher, having been referred by a mutual friend, called me in great distress because one of her students had lost a finger in an accident. My first question: "Are the other fingers intact and normal?" When she answered, "yes," I must confess that I almost responded, "What's the problem?" After all, I had never in my whole life enjoyed the luxury of nine normal fingers. Of course, I didn't say that. I expressed sympathy and concern for the student and described in some detail how I selected and adapted repertoire to compensate for my physical limitations. I tried to convince the teacher that with creativity, flexibility, patience, and optimism, the student would be able to continue playing the piano. I don't know the outcome of the situation; I hope that my counsel proved helpful and ultimately productive.

BALDWIN WALLACE HOSTED THE OHIO MUSIC TEACHERS ASSOCIATION state convention in September 1995. At the invitation of my colleague, Bob Mayerovitch, I presented a lecture/recital entitled, "Survival Strategies for the Physically Imperfect Pianist." After outlining my general philosophy, I presented specific examples, drawn from my "Romantic Miniatures," showing precisely how and why I had changed the execution of certain passages. In conclusion, I performed the pieces from which the examples had been taken.

Response to my presentation was overwhelmingly positive. Everyone agreed that my strategies, though necessarily tailored to my individual needs, represent a universally relevant approach, since all pianists at one time or another struggle with physical infirmity.

MY SUPPORT SYSTEM during the 1990s was a shifting landscape. When Gerri Jeris decided to resume selling real estate, Renie Martin, who now had her second little boy, became my driver for the next four years. In 1995, I met Sherrall Sadler, who had moved to Tower in the Park (from Georgia) to take care of her mother. Since her mother did not require constant care, Sherrall could drive me to and from the college, as well as to other appointments. I loved the convenience of having my driver in the building. By the time Sherrill's mother died, I had retired and no longer needed a regular driver. Throughout this period, my dear friend, Daniela Flandera, served in whatever capacity I needed her—grocery shopper, substitute driver, etc. I never worried; helpers seemed to materialize at just the right time.

THE FALL OF 1995 marked the beginning of my second three-year term as head of BW's piano department. I accepted the position cautiously, remembering that my first term had contributed to my physical collapse and the onset of rheumatoid arthritis. This time, however, I no longer carried a full teaching load. I also knew I'd be smart enough to delegate some of my administrative responsibilities, rather than trying to do everything myself—and the job now included $1,000 per year of additional compensation.

Prior to the start of the school year, the college sponsored a weekend retreat/workshop for incoming department heads and committee chairmen. Upon learning that we would be staying in scenic Amish country, about an hour's drive south of Berea, I signed up to attend, even though I didn't know how physically accessible the facilities might be.

I need not have worried. BW's associate dean, Carol Thompson, called me to say she had arranged for Chungsim Han, a young math professor, to be my roommate and helper for the weekend. Chungsim and I became instant friends. In later years, she would introduce me to her husband, Charlie Shalkhauser, her sister-in-law, Sue Grunau, and Sue's husband Mel. The five of us enjoyed many lovely dinners at Sue and Mel's home.

As a new department head, I was eligible to receive a computer, compliments of the college. Since I possessed "zero" computer skills, I nearly panicked when a couple of guys from the computer center plopped the monstrosity on my dining room table and said, "Here's your computer. Goodbye." Soon after that, Ruth Pickering gave me a cartoon depicting a dazed, befuddled Ziggy being taunted by his computer: "You don't have a clue what to do next, do you?" In desperation, I called the computer center for help, only to hear an unpleasant voice asking, "Where's your cursor?" I fought the strong temptation to shout, "NONE OF YOUR DAMN BUSINESS!" Instead, I swallowed my pride and stammered, "Wh-what's a cursor?" I thought I detected a groan at the other end of the line.

After arranging informal lessons with a member of the math and computer science faculty, I gradually learned to draft and print departmental memos, letters and jury schedules. My first relatively error-free memo prompted a congratulatory call from George Cherry: "Fantastic memo, Vickie!" I was still playing catch-up, but at least there were glimmers of progress.

PREPARATIONS FOR MY NEXT FACULTY RECITAL, scheduled for September 14, 1996, were briefly interrupted when, in early June, a tendon in the third finger of my left hand ruptured. After the intense pain subsided, I realized I could no longer lift that finger independently. I made an instantaneous decision not to seek medical attention. In fact, I didn't mention the incident to anyone. I simply took the pragmatic approach, went to the piano, and began testing myself to see if I could still play the repertoire I had been preparing for the recital—selections from Bartok's *For Children*, seven etudes by Stephen Heller (a contemporary of Chopin) and two pieces by the Mendelssohn siblings. To my great relief, I had to change only a few left-hand fingerings—the show would go on.

Despite a cold, rainy evening, an enthusiastic audience once again filled the chapel to capacity. My playing went very well, so afterward, I confessed the truth about my ruptured tendon to my colleagues. They all said, "I'm so glad I didn't know. I would've been terrified for you." That's exactly why I didn't tell them.

Feeling pleased and proud that I had managed to pull the rabbit out of the hat *one more time*, I was blissfully unaware that I had just presented my final piano performance.

The ruptured tendon proved to be a harbinger of things to come. By December, my left wrist and the middle joint of my left pinky finger were swollen and painful. I took a medical leave of absence for spring quarter; in mid-March 1997, Dr. Urbaniak stabilized the wrist and replaced my swollen fifth finger joint with a silicone implant. Despite the success of the surgery, I had to face a sobering fact: Never again would I be able to rely on my strong, dependable, "almost normal" left hand.

"THE TIMES—THEY WERE A-CHANGIN'." The conservatory had a new director. The college had switched from quarters to semesters. And with the deterioration of my left hand, I suspected that my performing career had ended. The spring of 1998 brought a mixture of relief and joy as I relinquished my department head duties and learned of my promotion to full professor. There was also a degree of sadness as George Cherry, my longtime colleague and friend, retired.

I spent my fall sabbatical in 1998 recovering from more hand surgery. In both of my fourth fingers, the joint nearest the nail had become squishy and sore. Fusion provided a relatively uncomplicated, permanent fix, although during the recuperation, I struggled with the inconvenience of having my hands simultaneously incapacitated. I had completed my official sabbatical project during the summer—an essay describing how I had maintained my career while coping with rheumatoid arthritis. *Piano and Keyboard* magazine eventually published a revised version of this article, "Understand and Manage Your Arthritis."

My best laugh that year came courtesy of Dady Mehta. His friend, Viennese composer Lucia Alcalay, in celebration of her seventieth birthday, had been asked to collect recordings of all her works to be placed in the Oesterreichische Nationalbibliothek. Dady sent her two tapes of the "Five Two-Voice Studies for Piano." His was made especially for the occasion; mine was from my 1968 St. Andrews performance. Guess what? She preferred mine! My "to do" list now includes going to Vienna to see for myself that a portion of my senior recital tape resides in the Austrian National Library.

UPON MY RETURN to campus in January 1999, I told Conservatory Director Catherine Jarjisian that I wanted to retire in December. I then made the announcement to my colleagues. The decision had been surprisingly easy. When I was initially diagnosed with RA, I knew that I wanted to keep doing as much as I could for as long as I could. Unquestionably, I had accomplished that goal. In fact, some of my most rewarding moments as teacher and performer had come in my post-arthritis years. I don't believe my students ever felt shortchanged because of my disability. Nevertheless, I had to acknowledge that they would benefit from having an able-bodied teacher who could demonstrate at the keyboard more readily than I. It seemed prudent to make my exit gracefully—and voluntarily.

FACULTY RECITAL AT BALDWIN-WALLACE COLLEGE

Kulas Musical Arts Building
Berea, Ohio
September 15, 1990

From "Little Piano Book" .... Vincent Persichetti
  Fanfare
  Lullaby
  Capriccio
  Dialogue
  Statement
  Arietta
  Humoreske
  Interlude
  Gloria
  Epilogue

Selected Piano Pieces .... Fanny Mendelssohn Hensel
  Andante cantabile
  O Dream of Youth, O Golden Star
  Nocturne

Three "Songs Without Words" .... Felix Mendelssohn
  Op. 102, No. 7 (Boat-Song)
  Op. 30, No. 6 (Boat-Song)
  Op. 30, No. 1 (Contemplation)

Note: I played this program in Bennettsville, S.C., in August 1991.

FACULTY RECITAL AT BALDWIN-WALLACE COLLEGE

Kulas Musical Arts Building
Berea, Ohio
September 19, 1992

From "For Children," Vol. I .... Bela Bartok
    (based on Hungarian Folk Tunes)
      No. 10 Allegro molto (Children's Dance)
      No. 11 Lento
      No. 8 Allegretto (Children's Game)
      No. 22 Allegretto
      No. 25 Parlando
      No. 26 Moderato
      No. 27 Allegramente (Jest)
      No. 28 Andante (Choral)
      No. 29 Allegro scherzando (Pentatonic Tune)
      No. 31 Andante tranquillo
      No. 32 Andante
      No. 36 Vivace (Drunkard's Song)

****

First Gymnopedie .... Erik Satie

From "Medusa's Trap" (7 Pieces for Piano)
      No. 1 Quadrillo
      No. 6 Polka
      No. 5 Un peu vif
      No. 3 Pas vite

From "Three Distinguished Waltzes of a Jaded Dandy"
  No. 2 "His Monocle"
  No. 3 "His Legs"

Third Gnossienne

****

"Farewell To Rome"
(Henle Ed., 1986) .... Fanny Mendelssohn Hensel

Two "Songs Without Words" .... Felix Mendelssohn
    Op. 62, No. 5 (Venetian Boat Song)
    Op. 62, No. 1 (May Breezes)

FACULTY RECITAL AT BALDWIN-WALLACE COLLEGE

Lindsay-Crossman Chapel
Berea, Ohio
September 17, 1994

"Romantic Miniatures"

From "Enfantines" .... Bloch
    Elves
    Pastorale
    Rainy Day
    The Joyous Party
    With Mother
    Teasing
    Melody

****

Dance of the Dragonflies .... Rohde

Requiem for a Little Bird .... Sandré

Prayer .... Fuchs

Cock-a-Doodle Waltz, Op. 243, No. 26 .... Kohler

Valsette, Op. 40, No. 1 .... Sibelius

Notturnino (from Album for the Young) .... Bossi

****

From "Trois Nouvelles Etudes" .... Chopin
    No. 1 in F Minor

Prelude in A Major, Op. 28, No. 7 .... Chopin

Song Without Words in A Major, Op. 102, No. 7 ..... Mendelssohn

Note: I played this program in Bennettsville, S.C., on March 23, 1995.

FACULTY RECITAL AT BALDWIN-WALLACE COLLEGE

Lindsay-Crossman Chapel
Berea, Ohio
September 14, 1996

From "For Children," Vol. I .... Bartok
  (based on Hungarian Folk Songs)
    No. 10 Children's Dance
    No. 25 Parlando
    No. 26 Moderato
    No. 27 Jest
    No. 28 Choral
    No. 29 Pentatonic Tune
    No. 31 Andante tranquillo
    No. 32 Andante
    No. 36 Drunkard's Song

Selected Etudes .... Heller
    D Major, Op. 125, No. 7
    B Minor, Op. 125, No. 8 (Da Capo No. 7)
    A Minor, Op. 125, No. 2
    B Minor, Op. 46, No. 11
    B-flat Major, Op. 125, No. 13
    D Minor, Op. 47, No. 10
    E Minor, Op. 47, No. 15

"O Dream of Youth, O Golden Star" .... Fanny M. Hensel

Song Without Words, Op. 62, No. 1 .... Felix Mendelssohn

UNDERSTAND AND MANAGE YOUR ARTHRITIS

(Published in the November/December 2000 issue of
Piano and Keyboard)

Chances are, every person reading this article either has some form of arthritis or knows someone who does. The more than 100 types of arthritis and related illnesses affect one of every seven people in the United States. Little is known about what causes most types of arthritis. The multitude of types suggests a multitude of causes.

The word *arthritis* is derived from the Greek word *arthron*, meaning "joint," and *itis*, meaning "inflammation." Since inflammation is not present in every form of arthritis, a more pragmatic definition might be "disease affecting the joints."

Arthritis is a complex illness because human joints, the parts of the body where bones meet, are complex structures with intricately interrelated parts. Cartilage, the gristly material on the ends of bones, acts as a buffer or shock absorber to prevent bone from rubbing against bone. The synovium, a capsule that encases the joint, secretes synovial fluid that lubricates the joint and facilitates movement. Muscles, elastic tissues that shorten or lengthen as needed, move bones—and you. Tendons are the fibrous cords that attach muscles to bones. Arthritis may affect one or more parts of a joint. Unfortunately, arthritis tends to be chronic, meaning that once you have it, you're likely to have it the rest of your life.

TYPES: Two common types of arthritis are osteoarthritis and rheumatoid arthritis. Osteoarthritis (OA) or "old age" arthritis is the most common, usually occurring in people 45 and older. By gradually breaking down the cartilage of the joint, OA leaves bones uncushioned, so that bone begins to rub against bone, causing pain and stiffness. OA involves no inflammation.

Rheumatoid arthritis (RA), on the other hand, begins with inflammation in the lining of the synovium, a process that appears to be caused by a malfunction in the body's immune system. Inflammatory cells divide and grow, causing swelling, pain, and a puffy appearance in the joint. Increased blood flow, due to the inflammation, may make the joint warm to the touch. The inflammatory cells do further damage by secreting enzymes that actually "eat away" cartilage and bone, and they may also threaten other parts of the joint. For unknown reasons, this most serious type of arthritis is much more common in women than in men.

An early diagnosis increases the chance that your arthritis can be controlled before significant joint damage has occurred. If you experience joint pain and stiffness lasting longer than two weeks, you should seek medical help. Your family doctor may be qualified to diagnose and treat your arthritis. If your hands and wrists are involved, however, it would be wise to consult a specialist, usually a rheumatologist, for a definitive diagnosis. Explain that you are a pianist and that *any* damage to your hands and wrists could seriously jeopardize your career. There is no cure for arthritis, but it can be successfully treated by a combination of medications, exercise, rest, and joint protection.

After determining that you have arthritis, and what type, your doctor should explain to you what medications are being prescribed, how and when to take them, how quickly they take effect, and what benefits—and side effects—you can expect. Ask questions if you are not provided with adequate information in any of these areas. Because so many medications are currently available and because each person's response is unique, you and your doctor will probably have to work together over a period of time to find the medications and dosages that are most effective for you.

EXERCISE: Both exercise and rest are essential and should be kept in balance. Sore, stiff joints will become even more stiff and painful if they are not exercised regularly. Done correctly, exercise helps to maintain and improve joint flexibility, strength, and function. Ask your doctor to recommend a good occupational therapist (OT) who can develop an exercise program that is appropriate for the type and severity of your arthritis.

Range-of-motion—or stretching exercises—are generally re-commended for all types of arthritis, even severe RA. "Stretching" means moving the joint as far as it will comfortably go (through its whole range of motion), then coaxing it a little farther, just past the point of discomfort. These exercises should be done gently, slowly, and *regularly.*

Tell your OT that you are a pianist because your exercise program should complement—and supplement—your practicing. Prior to exercising, you may want to apply moist heat (some people prefer cold) to your joints. If appropriate, your OT may also prescribe strengthening and endurance exercises.

What if you exercise and/or practice too much? The rule is that if exercise-induced pain lasts longer than two hours, cut back the next day, but don't stop exercising. *Never* take "extra" pain medication prior to exercising or practicing. Pain is the joint's way of protecting itself from overuse, and you need to know when you've had enough.

It takes time to find the right balance between exercise and rest, but, in my opinion, too much rest is preferable to too little. In addition to getting a good night's sleep, you must also pace your daytime activities. For pianists, this may mean shorter and/or fewer practice sessions, shorter and/or fewer performances, scheduling performances during times of least stress, and perhaps even a lighter teaching load. (All of these were necessary for me.)

If you listen to your body, your arthritic joints will tell you when and how much they need to rest. The best advice is to rest *before* you reach the point of severe fatigue.

PROTECTING YOURSELF: Joint protection means using your joints wisely so that excess stress and pain are avoided. My first OT gave me this example: "On any given day, there is only a limited amount of mileage you can expect from an arthritic joint, obviously *less* mileage than you would expect from a healthy joint. So, do you really want to spend that limited mileage pulling wet sheets out of a washer?" I got the message, of course, and immediately hired a household helper to do my laundry and cleaning!

After helping you identify those daily tasks and activities that are stressful to your joints, your OT can show you alternative ways of performing those tasks so that stress is reduced or eliminated. Some solutions are simple. If lifting a heavy drinking glass hurts your wrist, use a straw. If you feel a twinge of pain in your fingers every time you squeeze the toothpaste tube, set the tube on the counter and squeeze with your forearm. Your OT can also recommend a variety of assistive devices that can make your life easier. When there is no low-stress solution for a particular task or activity, you should avoid that task or activity, if at all possible. (Remember the wet sheets!)

PROTECTING YOURSELF AT THE KEYBOARD: Applying the principles of joint protection at the keyboard will likely mean changing not only *how much* you play, but also *what* and *how* you play.

Before selecting repertoire for performance, assess your physical limitations realistically and specifically, and then use those limitations as boundaries in the selection process. For example, if your left wrist hurts when you reach farther than a seventh, avoid pieces permeated with left-hand octaves. If your right fingers hurt in fast passagework, set aside that Mozart sonata.

This is *not* the time to stretch your technique. This *is* the time—and a golden opportunity—to search out those wonderful masterpieces that test your musical, not your physical, prowess.

After choosing repertoire, plan your physical execution of the piece in detail, to ensure that you're not using your arthritic joints in ways that unduly expose their weakness and vulnerability. For example, if your right index finger is sore and swollen, don't use it on notes that require heavy accents or delicate control. By using stronger, more dependable fingers in these crucial places, you will play more comfortably, confidently, and musically. And, equally important, you'll spare your arthritic joints unnecessary stress.

Finding the most comfortable (hence, musical) way of playing a piece may lead you into strange territory: highly unorthodox fingerings; playing notes with the left hand that would ordinarily be played with the right and vice versa; using hand-to-hand rather than finger-to-finger legato (one of my favorite strategies); even an occasional bit of "editing."

Any alteration of the score, of course, must be considered with great caution, but I have from time to time omitted the upper or lower notes of octaves and played hard-to-reach intervals melodically rather than harmonically, especially in an ac-companiment pattern. This kind of editing is justified only if the musical integrity of the piece is not violated, and if the musicality of the performance is enhanced.

My playing, before and after RA, has proved unequivocally that a performer can effectively communicate the musical content of a piece without playing every note exactly as it appears on the printed page. More than once I have been told, "If the composer had had your hands, the piece would have been written your way to start with!"

If (when) you encounter a piece that—despite all your ingenuity—you cannot play comfortably, don't perform it. Be a perfectionist. Your performances must sound as if you are

185

completely able-bodied.

MY CASE HISTORY: I was born with many malformed joints and have been in a wheelchair my entire adult life. Despite the small size of my right hand and limited mobility of my right wrist, I excelled pianistically, pursued my musical education, and joined the piano faculty at Baldwin-Wallace College in 1976. Because my physical condition was stable and painless, I regarded it as a mere "inconvenience."

In 1984, with the onset of rheumatoid arthritis, I began to regard myself as "disabled" for the first time. My right wrist succumbed almost immediately; surgery was necessary in 1985. In the following years, both hands deteriorated but very gradually. I continued to teach successfully, and by adapting my repertoire to each new limitation, I maintained my performing career through '96. After that, my hands deteriorated more rapidly. Surgery was necessary on my left wrist in '97, and on both fourth fingers in '98. I retired from teaching in December 1999.

I have now turned my energy to voice lessons (My farewell recital at Baldwin-Wallace was vocal!) and writing—or perhaps I should say "speaking," since I'm learning to use the voice-activation software on my new computer.

Understanding and managing your arthritis is a daunting task, but it *can* be done. By following the strategies I have outlined, I successfully maintained my career for fifteen years *after* becoming arthritic. Those of you who don't have the added burden of my complicated orthopedic history can expect to do much better!

RESOURCES

* Statistical and medical information used in this article was provided by the Northeastern Ohio Chapter of the Arthritis Foundation (AF).

* A wealth of information is available at the AF website (www.arthritis.org).

A LESSON IN REALITY

Many able-bodied children are understandably fascinated and puzzled by their first encounter with a person in a wheelchair. Through the years, I've cheerfully answered a variety of questions:

"Why can't you walk?"

"What happened to your legs?"

"Can you do stuff like regular people?"

I've always been glad that children find me approachable because it's important for them to learn that people with disabilities are a part of reality and that most of us manage, though perhaps in irregular ways, to "do stuff like regular people."

My favorite incident occurred at the country club swimming pool in Bennettsville. Wheeling toward the shallow end of the pool, I noticed that a perky five-or six-year-old girl, already in the water, was watching me intently.

"Why are you ridin' around in that wheelbarrow?" she blurted out.

I smiled, explaining the difference between the *barrow* and the *chair* and why I had to use the latter. Not moving a muscle, she accepted my explanation without comment. I removed my shoes and prepared to lower myself into the water.

"That sure is a funny lookin' toe!"

I smiled again, finding it both heartwarming and amusing that she had overlooked all of my more obvious deformities and had zeroed in on the one truly unique and interesting oddity of my appearance—the fourth toe on my left foot. This tiny, pathetic appendage never grew beyond its "Little Piggy" stage. It sits slightly forward on my foot, not in line with the other toes, and is further distinguished by a small wrinkle at its base with just a hint of a toenail. I've always assumed that because my foot was often in surgical casts during my childhood years, the toe simply did not have enough room for normal growth.

After congratulating my young friend on her keen powers of observation, I explained these circumstances as best I could. Seemingly satisfied, she swam away.

For the next half hour, I concentrated on my exercises and was therefore taken off guard by the insistent little voice behind me:

"Can I see that funny lookin' toe again?"

"Of course you can!" This time I could not contain my laughter as I allowed my left foot to float to the surface.

After several long seconds of uninterrupted staring, she apparently reassured herself that she hadn't been seeing things the first time.

"Bye!" she said, rejoining her friends.

Whenever I'm inclined to take myself—or my troubles—too seriously, I think of that delightful little girl, in whose eyes I was the lady in a wheelbarrow with a funny lookin' toe that had to be seen twice to be believed.

I think we both learned a lesson in reality that day.

A SEASON TO SING

DURING SPRING BREAK 1999, I was at Fay McLaurin's house one afternoon, bemoaning the fact that I couldn't *play* a farewell recital at BW. She immediately suggested that I go back to my musical roots and sing! When I protested, citing my meager vocal training, she said with complete confidence that she would help me assemble "a delightful program of folk songs and spirituals," the kind of music I had performed successfully as an adolescent.

I remained unconvinced. After all, my professional credits were entirely pianistic; as a singer, I was strictly an amateur. Consequently, I would have to be careful to avoid even the slightest hint of pretentiousness. The very thought of scheduling a "voice recital" seemed presumptuous.

Fay agreed, but stuck to her guns. As we continued to talk, the project gradually took shape. She suggested calling the program "A Season To Sing." I suggested placing this Bible verse from Ecclesiastes on the inside page of the printed program: "To everything there is a season, and a time to every purpose under heaven." Since I felt comfortable speaking to my audiences, I would simply explain at the outset that I wanted to say farewell and that I wanted to do it in a musical way. Given the deterioration of my hands (which my listeners were well aware of), I had chosen the only other performing medium open to me.

By the end of spring break, Fay and I had selected four folk songs and four spirituals that were attractive, varied, and vocally uncomplicated. Fay located a book that contained historical commentary about the music. The final, crucial detail fell into place when my friend Josie Harris, a member of BW's adjunct piano faculty, agreed to be my accompanist.

A standing-room-only crowd gathered in the chapel on the evening of September 11, 1999, to hear my farewell performance. Over the years, I had encountered a variety of pre-recital crises— upset stomach, nosebleed, etc. This time, however, the problem involved my wheelchair. At 7:40 p.m., I was on the lower level of the chapel, trying to stay calm and collected. (The perform- ance would be upstairs in the sanctuary.) As I made my way to the elevator, the rubber rim on the left wheel of my chair simply fell off! I screamed, watching in horror. With the wheel spinning uselessly in space, I couldn't possibly maneuver the chair onto the stage. So much for staying calm and collected.

The look on my stage manager's face told me he would be no help whatsoever. Fortunately, my aide, Sherrall Sadler, a woman of remarkable resourcefulness, was with me. Her past careers had run the gamut from truck driver to jewelry store owner. That night, she added "wheelchair repair" to her resume as she pulled a little implement of some sort from her purse and began matter- of-factly reattaching the rim to the wheel. Problem solved! There were no further mishaps, although Sherrall, who sat on the front row of the sanctuary, had a worried look on her face whenever I had to maneuver the chair.

In keeping with the farewell nature of the occasion, prior to the last song on the program, I reminisced about my twenty-three years at BW:

"IN LIGHT OF MY UPCOMING RETIREMENT, I'd like to offer a few personal reflections before concluding tonight's program.

"Throughout my twenty-three years at Baldwin Wallace, my physical circumstances have been, to say the least, less than ideal.

When I came to BW in the fall of 1976, there was no elevator in Kulas [the building where I taught]; since my teaching involved the Piano Lab, which is housed on the second floor, I had to be carried up and down the stairs every day. I knew that an elevator would be installed eventually. I'm glad I didn't know that 'eventually' was ten years away!

"And there were the Cleveland winters. My first two winters here were 1977 and 1978 [groans and laughs from the older members of the audience], which, as some of you know, broke records for snowfall and for the number of consecutive days with temperatures below zero. Of course, after surviving those two seasons, I figured I could survive just about anything.

"Then, worst of all, in 1984, I experienced the onset of rheumatoid arthritis, which transformed my physical disability from the stable, painless condition I had been born with—and which I had always regarded as a mere inconvenience—into a chronic, progressive disorder that jeopardized my health and resulted in the gradual deterioration of my hands.

"So why did I choose to stay at BW for twenty-three years? There is a simple, one-word answer: *people*. I learned very quickly that BW is a special place because of its people. Here I found colleagues whose level of expertise inspired me to the highest standards of professionalism. Here I found students whose enthusiasm and dedication—or, in a few cases—whose *lack of* enthusiasm and dedication [chuckles from the audience] challenged me to be the best teacher I could be. And here I found loyal, loving friends who have been willing to go *two* extra miles to help and support me in whatever ways were needed.

"What will I remember about my twenty-three years at BW? Don't worry, this isn't an exhaustive list.

"I'll remember the student who said, 'Thank you for teaching me to love the piano.' And I'll remember the student who said,

'This is the only class I don't fall asleep in.'

"I'll remember that during those ten long years of being carried up and down the stairs in Kulas, I never got dropped—not even once. There were, however, one or two anxious moments.

"I'll remember that in 1997, when I needed to have surgery on my left wrist, my piano department colleagues said, 'Never mind that it's the middle of the school year. You should request a leave of absence and have the surgery as soon as possible.' I did, and the surgery succeeded in stabilizing my wrist.

"I'll remember those embarrassing moments during my early years at BW when I was mistaken for a student. The head of the piano department at that time, Evelyn Gott, invited me out to dinner; and when I ordered a glass of wine with my meal, the waitress asked to see my ID. Several years later, I was at a recital and was introduced to a woman who wanted to know how long I'd been at BW. I said, 'This is my fourth year.' Without a moment's pause, she asked me very sweetly, 'What do you plan to do after graduation?' [loud laughter]

"I'll remember the satisfaction of seeing students mature, graduate, and establish themselves professionally.

"And, of course, I'll always remember and be grateful that the people at BW chose to see my abilities, not my *disability*.

"About a year ago, a former student wrote me a letter, which began: 'Dear Dr. Covington, you have the most adventurous life of anyone I know.' I do consider my years at BW to have been a great adventure, and as I approach retirement, I want to assure you that my spirit of adventure is alive and well. Although it has become necessary for me to bring to a close the pianistic chapter of my life, I look forward to 'A Season to Sing' and 'A Season to Write' and seasons for other adventures I haven't even thought of yet.

"I'd like to conclude these remarks by sharing with you a few lines from Alfred, Lord Tennyson. I came across these lines quite by chance in a book called *A Poem a Day*. Upon reading them, I knew instantly that they expressed how I view my present situation and the perspective I aspire to as I look to the future:

> *Though much is taken, much abides; and though*
> *We are not now that strength which in old days*
> *Moved earth and heaven; that which we are, we are;*
> *One equal temper of heroic hearts,*
> *Made weak by time and fate, but strong in will*
> *To strive, to seek, to find, and not to yield."*

The final song—a lovely, lyrical arrangement of *This Little Light of Mine (I'm Gonna Let It Shine)*—drew thunderous applause and a standing ovation. Never have I felt more in touch with an audience than I did that night.

Virtually everyone stayed to greet me after the recital. Some of the comments touched me deeply, such as Bob Mayerovitch's obviously heartfelt assertion that he heard in my singing the same elements of artistry and musicianship that he had always admired in my playing. Others made me laugh out loud, especially Jim Feldman's impish remark (which he whispered in my ear), "I think there's a place for you in Vegas."

I had not seen Ray Kubacki since the death of his wife and had feared his own declining health would prevent him from attending the recital. How happy I was that one of his daughters brought him. Instantly renewing our friendship, we enjoyed periodic lunch dates for the next several years, until he had to move to assisted living.

I got my biggest surprise of the evening when one of my favorite former students, whom I had not seen since 1983, appeared. I had "discovered" John Mramor, a composition/tuba major, in one of my beginning level piano classes. Recognizing his exceptional attitude and aptitude, I quickly persuaded him to become a composition/piano major. Professionally, he'd been a joy to work with; personally, I had always thought I'd like to have him as a friend someday. Now, as if by magic, he stood before me, giving me that long-awaited opportunity.

John told me that after the completion of his master's in music theory and composition at Kent State University, he had served as a church music director for a time. Then he decided to become a licensed massage therapist. He currently served in that capacity at a local hospice facility for the homeless. He promised that when I returned to Berea in the spring (after spending the winter in South Carolina), we would get together—and we did.

By 10:30 p.m., the last well-wisher had left. I felt both physically exhausted and emotionally exhilarated, the events of the evening racing furiously through my mind. At that moment, I realized that I owed these cherished memories to the wisdom and foresight of Fay McLaurin. What fun I had the next day sharing with her by phone every detail.

FAREWELL RECITAL
AT BALDWIN-WALLACE COLLEGE
WITH JOSIE HARMON HARRIS, PIANIST

"A Season To Sing"

Lindsay-Crossman Chapel
Berea, Ohio
September 11, 1999

"Folk Songs and Spirituals of North America"

Johnny Has Gone for a Soldier .... Northern U.S.

The Little Horses (from Old American Songs) .... Southern U.S.
Arr. Aaron Copland

The Housewife's Lament .... Northern U.S.

Young Charlotte .... Northern U.S.

Steal Away to Heaven .... Trad. Spirituals
Nobody Knows the Trouble I've Seen .... Arr. Mark Hayes
Sometimes I Feel Like a Motherless Child
Steal Away

Personal Reflections on My Years at Baldwin-Wallace College

This Little Light of Mine
   (I'm Gonna Let It Shine) .... Trad. Spiritual
                                                          Arr. Hale Smith

Note: I presented this program with Fay McLaurin at the Marlboro Civic Center in Bennettsville, S.C., on August 20, 2000. As an encore, I sang "Over the Rainbow."

CHAPTER THIRTEEN

LOSING MOTHER TO ALZHEIMER'S

THE LAST YEARS OF MY COLLEGE TEACHING CAREER coincided with Mother's slow, inevitable descent into Alzheimer's disease. Preliminary symptoms began in the early 1990s: brief lapses of judgment, disorientation, moments when her behavior seemed not quite "right." Next came episodes of short-term memory loss. When she started forgetting tennis dates, I knew something had to be done.

I persuaded Mother to go to a local doctor, ostensibly for a checkup. Since tests revealed no other explanation for the memory problems, he prescribed Aricept. I firmly believe that early intervention and continued medical supervision were crucial factors in Mother's longevity. She lived with Alzheimer's for about fifteen years, and, for most of that time, she functioned fairly well. Of course, I also credit her tenacity and courage. She fought for her life every step of the way.

IN MID-AUGUST 1994, Mother learned that she would be inducted into the South Carolina Tennis Hall of Fame. When she received the call informing her of the honor, I was lying on her bed watching TV. I heard her say, "You mean I actually *won?*" I let out a scream so loud it might have been heard in Bennettsville four miles away.

The awards banquet took place at Kiawah Island near Charleston on December 3, one day after Mother's seventy-sixth birthday. Many of her tennis friends and doubles partners attended, although Mother was particularly pleased by the presence of John Fowler, who had first played with her in the 1930s at Furman University. They were ranked number one in South Carolina 65 mixed doubles for six straight years (1987-92). I had helped Mother with her acceptance speech, which she delivered smoothly and flawlessly. I'm sure that only her family and closest friends were aware of her incipient Alzheimer's.

The next fall, my duties at Baldwin Wallace prevented me from attending Mother's induction into the Athletic Hall of Fame at her alma mater, Furman University, in Greenville, South Carolina. I did, however, go shopping with her for snazzy new outfits to wear during the festivities.

BEFORE ALZHEIMER'S, Mother had been the very person-ification of efficiency and organization; consequently, as she became aware of her mental decline, her frustration level increased. During my vacation periods in Bennettsville, I did everything I could to assist her in planning meals, remembering appointments, and other such tasks. In one poignant letter (written after I had returned to Ohio), she thanked me for my help, adding that she hoped she wasn't being a burden by leaning on me too much. I responded immediately that *no way* could she ever be a burden to me and that after all the years when I had leaned on her, I was more than happy to return the favor.

In a letter dated January 2, 1998—at which point Mother's Alzheimer's would have been classified as moderate—she could still express herself clearly and coherently:

> *Dearest Vickie,*
>
> *Harry and I were glad to learn that you arrived back in Berea safely and that your flight went well. The house will seem very lonesome for quite a while, but the few weeks you spent with us were filled with much pleasure*

and enjoyment that will linger for quite a while! I hope you found everything intact in your abode and that you won't be too tired when you get back into your school routine. You can rest assured that we will treasure the short weeks you spent here in the country! I will be going to bed soon, but just wanted to tell you once again how much it means to us for you to spend your holidays with us. Give my kindest regards to Ruth [Pickering], Lue [Fletcher], and all of your wonderful friends. I hope their vacation was very enjoyable.

I'll write again soon, but just want to let you know that your vacation was a treat for your Mom and Dad!
Dearest love,
Mother

Mother's deterioration was very gradual, but eventually, she needed more doctors and more medications. Like other families facing Alzheimer's, we scoured the literature for information about possible new treatments, but every tantalizing breakthrough in research seemed to carry the disheartening conclusion that "application" and "general use" were years away, in other words, too far in the future to help Mother.

For family members, sometimes the best medicine is a large dose of laughter combined with a healthy appreciation for the ridiculous. A friend of mine, whose mother had Alzheimer's, told me that one day his mother asked him to drive her car to the grocery store to get a few items for her. Shortly after he left, she called the local police and reported that her car had been stolen!

Mother's behavior, although never that extreme, could be frustrating and annoying. Since telephone conversations tended to confuse her, Daddy and I tried to intercept incoming calls, but no plan is foolproof. Once when Mother answered the phone, I could tell she was talking to someone about our long-distance service. "Well, we really don't make very many long-distance calls," she said tentatively. I urged her to hang up, but she seemed intent on prolonging the conversation. Suddenly, her whole demeanor changed: "Wait a minute. I don't even live here. You'd better call back later." How I would love to have seen the look on that telemarketer's face.

A RELATIVELY MINOR MEDICAL PROBLEM can become a full-blown crisis when Alzheimer's is added to the equation. The cause of Mother's severe abdominal pain in early November 1999 turned out to be scar tissue that had somehow become wrapped around her colon, creating a blockage. Following successful surgery, Mother's recovery seemed assured. The hospitalization, however, sent her into a mental tail-spin; she absolutely refused to eat.

For reasons that are still unclear to me, after being released by the surgeon, Mother was transferred to the psychiatric wing of the Bennettsville hospital. As soon as she began to eat normally, she could go home; but she continued to abstain. The stalemate dragged on for at least a week. Mary Jo kept me abreast of these developments by telephone. At that point, I wanted nothing more than to finish my last semester of teaching at BW. When I asked Mary Jo why Daddy didn't take charge of the situation and insist that Mother be allowed to go home, she told me that he had said, "Maybe Vickie will come and know what to do." I think fear and worry had rendered him incapable of making a decision.

FLYING TO SOUTH CAROLINA the day before Thanksgiving, I was a woman on a mission. I had already asked Mary Jo to set up an appointment for me with Mother's psychiatrist Friday morning. Mentally preparing my arguments, I knew I had to be lucid, logical, and persuasive. Antagonizing him would be counterproductive, so I had vetoed the part where I questioned the validity of his medical credentials.

Daddy seemed genuinely comforted by my presence and open to any advice I might give. When I suggested that we hire someone to help with Mother's care after she came home from the hospital, he did not object. We first called the woman who had taken care of me after my left wrist surgery in 1997. She was not available, but she recommended Mrs. Josephine McCollum, who lived in Bennettsville and had experience with Alzheimer's patients. Josephine said she'd come to our house Saturday afternoon for an interview. Things were falling into place, but the main purpose of the trip still lay before me.

I usually smile when meeting someone for the first time, but I did not smile at Dr. Cahn. His first words to me were, "You must be the music professor from Ohio." I replied as sternly as I dared, "That's right." Without preamble, I began stating, calmly but emphatically, the reasons why Mother should be allowed to go home ASAP. I pointed out that if Mother did go home and still refused to eat, we could decide what to do next—but I believed that in familiar surroundings, she'd resume her normal activities, like eating. Dr. Cahn said he'd release Mother the next morning.

Daddy brought Mother and me home and left to go to the grocery store. After she and I had chatted in the den for a while, I suggested casually, although I could feel my heart pounding in my ears, "It's about lunchtime. Why don't we go to the kitchen and find something to eat?" "Okay." I had never heard a sweeter one-word answer. Jack had placed a container of his homemade vegetable beef soup in the refrigerator. Mother heated a small amount, and we each ate a bowl with Saltine crackers. When Daddy returned, I greeted him with the wonderful news. He burst into tears.

Josephine impressed Daddy and me with her kindness, competence, pleasant personality, and flexibility. She seemed willing to do whatever might be required to take care of Mother. Her previous Alzheimer's patient, who had exhibited severe behavioral problems, had taught her the value of rolling with the punches, something Daddy and I were just beginning to learn. We hired Josephine for a trial period of two weeks; she served faithfully as the mainstay of my parents' support system for nearly eleven years.

Since Mother had always done her own cooking and household chores, we had no idea how she would react to Josephine's presence. I remember Daddy saying, "I don't think you'll have to worry about violence or cursing, but she may fuss—*a lot.*" Josephine assured us it would take more than fussing to ruffle her feathers.

Boarding the plane for Cleveland on Sunday afternoon, I heaved a sigh of relief: *Mission accomplished.*

WITH THE CLOSE OF MY FINAL SEMESTER AT BW, the reality of my retirement began to sink in. I had felt no compulsion in making my decision, and I never had any regrets or second thoughts. From the moment I had been diagnosed with RA, I knew I was on borrowed time. I had maintained my career for fifteen years after that diagnosis, a phenomenal achievement, according to my rheumatologist. Now, at age fifty-three, with only a slight twinge of sadness, I declared myself "disabled" and applied for Social Security Disability Income (SSDI). I planned to keep my apartment in Berea, dividing my time between Ohio and South Carolina, making sure I spent every winter down South.

In some respects, I looked forward to retirement. I wanted to take full advantage of whatever good years Mother had left, and I sensed that Daddy would increasingly rely on my input as he made decisions about Mother's care.

TO MY DELIGHT, Jim Feldman "emceed" my retirement

202

reception at the Conservatory in early December. After making appropriately complimentary remarks about my musical and pedagogical skills, he moved on to my "Southern grace and charm," which, he said, I had impeccably transplanted to my Midwest environment.

"I think the time has come," he concluded, "for a remake of *Gone With The Wind* [dramatic pause] with Vickie, of course, as Scarlett O'Hara [another dramatic pause] and me as Rhett Butler."

This drew chuckles from the audience primarily because Jim's diminutive height and slight build made him the total opposite of Clark Gable. "Last night," Jim continued, "when I shared this idea with my wife, she expressed her strong disapproval, to which I responded, 'Frankly, my dear, I don't give a damn!'"

Laughter and applause engulfed the room. When at last I had composed myself, I enthusiastically accepted his invitation: "Let's do it, Jim! I'm ready whenever you are!"

"SMOOTH SAILING" best describes my first year of retirement. Mother's condition presented no new problems, and Josephine's expertise in managing the household gave Daddy substantial blocks of time to do errands, tend to his garden, or just relax and take a nap without worrying about Mother.

When I arrived in Bennettsville for the winter of 2000, Josephine said that Mother's initial greeting to her had been brusque and direct: "What are you doing in my kitchen?" Mother had never been inclined to beat around the bush.

"Well, Miz Covington," (No true Southerner ever pronounces a married woman's title with two syllables.) Mr. Covington thought you could use a little help."

"I don't need any help." But she had made no further protest and seemed to accept Josephine's presence as natural and normal.

Unfortunately, Daddy and I had neglected to tell Josephine about

Mother's habit of walking out to the edge of the front yard to pick up trash and pull weeds. We had not discouraged this activity because Mother was sufficiently alert not to get too close to the highway, and it seemed to be a harmless way of occupying her time and energy.

One morning, Josephine looked out the dining room window, saw Mother, and immediately assumed her to be in grave danger: "Lord, have mercy! Miz Covington's gonna get run over!" Josephine panicked and went racing across the yard, screaming, "Miz Covington, Miz Covington, get back in the house!"

Mother put her hand on her hip and retorted: "No! You have your job to do, and I have mine."

Frustrated and still quite alarmed, Josephine went to wake up Daddy, who was snoozing in the den. "There's no need to worry," he told her calmly. "Chris does this all the time. Just keep an eye on her." Josephine says that even recalling this incident elevates her blood pressure.

WITH THE NEW MILLENNIUM CAME THE NEW ADVENTURE of joining the choir at Trinity United Methodist Church in Clio, South Carolina, where Fay McLaurin serves as organist and music director. Fay had been persistent in recruiting me, but I hadn't needed much persuading. Since Clio is located on Highway 9, about three miles beyond my parents' house, Fay had been quick to point out that transportation would be no problem. I could ride with her coming and going.

Fay had told me that the choir, although small, was dedicated to musical excellence. Everyone welcomed me royally from the beginning; I, in turn, considered it a privilege to be a part of the group. In addition to my singing with the choir, Fay soon had me learning solos and participating in vocal duets—the icing on the cake. Over the next six years, I formed and renewed friendships with many kind, generous people, who made my "Trinity experience" extraordinarily satisfying.

Almost as soon as Fay learned of my successful farewell recital at BW, which she had masterminded, she began hatching an ambitious follow-up plan, namely, that she and I should perform the same program in Bennettsville at the Marlboro Civic Center. I agreed, but first, I had an ambitious plan of my own: to return to Ohio and study voice with Greg Upton, BW's staff accompanist and vocal coach. Greg had given me excellent last-minute pointers prior to my farewell recital and had expressed willingness to teach me on a regular basis after my retirement.

THE SPRING AND EARLY SUMMER of 2000 offered a delightful array of activities as I returned to Berea for the first time as a retiree. My friends were eager to celebrate my new title, *professor emerita*. As we sampled one restaurant after another, Renie Martin observed brilliantly and accurately: "Vickie, I think your favorite hobby is going out to lunch!" Josie Harris and I frequently combined lunch with shopping sprees at the mall. John Mramor gave me a personal tour of the hospice facility for the homeless where he worked as massage therapist. I joined the local recreation center so I could walk in the indoor pool a few days a week. Frieda Overton, a neighbor and friend at Tower in the Park, became the latest in a long line of loyal, able helpers. I began using the Jitney, a marvelous transportation service for the elderly and disabled, which cost only a dollar a ride. With every aspect of my life going smoothly, I began to wonder why I had not retired sooner.

Studying with Greg Upton yielded remarkable results. As my technique improved, the emerging resonance and richness of my voice amazed me. Sometimes at my lessons, I would sing only a few notes before Greg stopped me and said, "No, you're not doing it right." I'd be allowed to continue the song only when I was doing it right.

After my retirement, Dady and Martha Mehta frequently drove to Berea to see me. We'd usually go to lunch, followed by a visit to one of Cleveland's fascinating museums. Our excursions gradually became more ambitious. On an overnight visit to the famous glass museum in Corning, New York, their dear friend, Marilyn Meeker, accompanied us and served as my roommate and helper at the hotel. On this trip, I discovered Marilyn's encyclopedic knowledge of thoroughbred racing. She stupefied me with her ability to quote chapter-and-verse statistics concerning every Triple Crown Champion. Marilyn was once again my companion when, for our grand finale, we traveled to Pittsburgh to hear the Mehtas' younger son, Bejun, a world-renowned operatic countertenor, sing the title role in Handel's *Julius Caesar*.

Inspired by a biography of astrophysicist Stephen Hawking (given to me by the Mehtas), I launched a reading project of exploring and attempting to comprehend the leading scientific theories about the structure and laws of the universe. From there, I branched out into the relationship between science and religion. The more I read, the more engrossed I became. Needless to say, this is an ongoing, lifetime project. I'm hoping for definitive answers beyond the grave.

FAY McLAURIN AND I TOOK THE STAGE of the Marlboro Civic Center in Bennettsville on Sunday afternoon, August 20, 2000, to present "A Season To Sing." My confidence level had seldom been higher. Thanks to Greg Upton, I had successfully reinvented myself as a singer. Moreover, unlike my BW farewell, which had been inevitably tinged with nostalgic, bittersweet elements, my civic center recital was an entirely joyous celebration, a true beginning.

Several times in the weeks preceding the performance, Daddy suggested that I sing *Over the Rainbow*, a favorite during my teenage years, for an encore. I had initially nixed the idea: "*Over the Rainbow* is a good song," I tried to explain logically, "but it's not a folk song or a spiritual, so it really won't fit in with the rest of program." I could tell he was unconvinced.

About forty-eight hours before show time, Fay and I decided that pleasing Daddy took precedence over programmatic continuity. My encore, however, would be a surprise to everyone, including Daddy. When the time came, I just said, "This is a song I enjoyed singing as a young girl. I'd like to dedicate it to my dad." Fay gave me only an arpeggio as an introduction. With the opening notes, "Some—where," there were murmurs of recognition, followed by a ripple of applause from the audience. My voice wobbled for an instant, but I quickly recovered. The conclusion, "If happy little bluebirds fly beyond the rainbow, why—oh why—can't I?" was greeted with cheers and a standing ovation.

At the reception, Daddy approached me, grinning from ear to ear, and gave me a big kiss. Sometimes a "misfit" encore is exactly right.

ON FRIDAY, SEPTEMBER 8, having barely recovered from the recital, I flew to Champaign for four wonderful days at the University of Illinois, my old stomping ground. I stayed at a hotel on campus so I'd be accessible to everyone I wanted to see.

Dean Sanders had very kindly volunteered to provide transportation as needed throughout my visit. On the first day, he took me to see my dear friend, Barb Bauer. Though thin and frail, her inner spirit remained radiant. Knowing that in recent years Barb had become an accomplished designer of authentic period costumes for Barbie dolls, I eagerly anticipated seeing her collection—but I anticipated even more eagerly seeing the Fanny Mendelssohn doll that she would be presenting to me in commemoration of my recent retirement.

I was not disappointed. The gorgeous pink taffeta gown with coordinating cape and bonnet literally made me gasp. In keeping with Fanny's Jewish heritage, Barb had even found a brunette, brown-eyed Barbie. Barb's generosity and scrupulous attention to detail deeply touched me. We spent our time together happily reminiscing and catching up on each other's lives.

On Saturday afternoon, Dean offered to take Nancy Stagg and me to Arcola, Illinois, for the famous Broom Corn Festival Parade, featuring the equally famous Lawn Rangers, who, according to Dean, were considered by many observers, "who had had a couple of beers," to be the finest precision lawn mower drill team in the world. He informed us that the group's motto is, "You're only young once, but you can always be immature." Nancy and I were not going to pass up this unique opportunity. The entire parade, including the Lawn Rangers, proved to be a delightful slice of Midwestern Americana. Afterward, we returned to Champaign for a delicious dinner at a Mexican restaurant.

Mr. Konitzki came to the hotel Sunday morning and treated me to breakfast. He looked a bit older, but his warmth and charm were undimmed. Laughingly, we recalled my early days at the university, when I had been a "scared little kid." I thanked him for his help during that difficult period of adjustment and also for his subsequent audacity in nominating me for the Medallion of Honor. I owed "Mr. K." an enormous debt of gratitude—yet here he was, treating me to breakfast.

Later in the day, Nancy and I made an enjoyable excursion to Allerton Park, which Tom Baker and I had so memorably explored some thirty years earlier. I considered it to be truly hallowed ground. Since Nancy is one of the few people I can talk to about my efforts to understand the universe, we had a lively discussion, sharing ideas and recommending books to each other. "You'll never stop being a student!" she chuckled.

Dr. Leonhard invited me to lunch on Monday at his retirement community. He expressed pride in my successful career, adding that he felt deeply gratified to have played a role in my professional development. I wished him a happy eightieth birthday (which would be in December) and was saddened to learn that he died just a few months after his celebratory bash.

When I called Martin Cox, my favorite bus driver, his wife, Jackie, told me that for several months, he had been a patient in the VA hospital in Danville, Illinois. I am truly grateful that Dean insisted on driving me there. As I entered Martin's room, I could hardly believe my eyes. He looked emaciated and shrunken, a shadow of his former self. His face brightened when he saw me: "Don't tell me—Vickie, Vickie Covington?" I hugged him and introduced him to Dean, who discreetly made his exit.

Despite his weakened condition, traces of the old Martin remained. We chatted about mutual friends and acquaintances, including my former roommate, Phyllis Goren. He remembered her fondly and was sorry to hear of her death. When I questioned Martin about his care in the VA hospital, tears rolled down his cheeks. "This is a terrible place, Vickie. It's like being in prison." I felt utterly heartbroken and powerless to do anything for him. I could only hug him, tell him how much I loved him and that I'd pray for him to be released from the hospital soon.

Martin did go home before Christmas, but he died the following April. Jackie sent me a copy of the obituary and a lovely letter, in which she gave me these comforting words: "Martin really cared for you, Vickie. He spoke of you often and was as proud of you and your accomplishments as your own family is. Take care of yourself and keep on doing good things. I know Martin is looking down from heaven with all the angels and still looking out for us as he always did."

WITHIN SIX MONTHS of my return from Illinois, Mother's mental capacity had noticeably diminished—no more smooth sailing. One day we were talking about my retirement from Baldwin Wallace. "What did you teach?" she asked. I barely managed to remain calm. I said, "I taught piano there for over twenty years." Her response: "That's wonderful. I'm so proud of you." There would be many such heart-rending moments.

Daddy suffered a heart attack on July 21, 2001. After being stabilized at the Bennettsville hospital, he went by ambulance to a hospital in Florence, where he remained in the cardiac care unit for ten days. His doctors implanted a stent in his clogged artery and gave him an encouraging prognosis.

Mother and I made the hour-long drive to Florence every day to see Daddy. She drove; I navigated. My nerves began to wear a little thin, hearing her say *every day* that she hadn't been on that road in a long time. Once we arrived back home, she'd start asking questions about Daddy. I'd say that he had been hospitalized in Florence. She'd exclaim, "Let's go see him!" I'd explain that we had just returned from seeing him, which would satisfy her momentarily. Then she'd ask me *again* where Daddy was. I became almost envious of her capacity to "forget."

Daddy had barely recovered when, in early September, I had a gallbladder attack. A surgeon at the Bennettsville hospital removed both my gallbladder and appendix, a seemingly routine procedure.

Within two days of leaving the hospital, however, I had a fever and more abdominal pain. According to the Bennettsville surgeon, these symptoms were caused by diverticulitis. When he recommended immediate surgery to remove part of my colon,

Daddy cautioned, "Wait a minute. Let's get a second opinion." Since he had been favorably impressed with the medical care he had received at the hospital in Pinehurst, North Carolina, we requested that I be taken there.

On the morning of September 11, 2001, an ambulance took me to the Pinehurst hospital. Upon arrival, I heard strange, incredible stories about a terrorist attack in New York City, planes flying into buildings, and thousands of people being killed. Even after I turned on the TV in my room, I could scarcely comprehend what had happened. I recall clearly following these horrible events as I lay in my bed.

Tests showed my problem to be not diverticulitis, but an infection of the colon, *Clostridium difficile*, better known as C-diff. My Pinehurst doctor said I had probably contracted the infection in the Bennettsville hospital: The antibiotics given to me after my gallbladder surgery had upset the balance of "good" and "bad" bacteria in my colon, allowing the C-diff bacteria to take over.

Over the next four months, I was hospitalized in Pinehurst four times for at least a week each time. After being treated with antibiotics, my symptoms would subside. I'd go home, but a week later—or two weeks later—I'd be back in the hospital, testing positive for C-diff.

At first mystified, my doctor eventually concluded that the underlying problem was my rheumatoid arthritis, which alters the body's immune system. Because the drugs used to treat RA suppress the immune system, he felt he had no choice but to take me off of all my arthritis medications.

With my fourth hospitalization, my gastroenterologist offered to send me to Duke University Medical Center but added that he did have one more strategy in mind. I found the prospect of going to Duke so daunting that I agreed wearily to go along with his two-step plan.

Step One: I would undergo a colonoscopy to rid my system of as much infection as possible. Since I was too nauseous to swallow the "prep," my doctor placed a tube through my nose, down my throat, and into my stomach. The nurses literally poured the prep into me. Resisting the urge to throw up during this process took all my powers of concentration, leaving me physically weak and emotionally exhausted.

Step Two: I would take vancomycin, a powerful antibiotic known to be highly effective in curing C-diff. This regimen began immediately after the colonoscopy. By the time I left the hospital, the symptoms of my colon infection had subsided, but my arthritic joints hurt so intensely that I could scarcely move. Only a hefty dose of prednisone, prescribed by my rheumatologist, put me back on my feet.

I systematically reduced my dosage of vancomycin over the next three months until at the end I took one tablet every third day. The C-diff never recurred; however, my joy and relief were tempered by a keen awareness of my vulnerability to infection and the complicating role RA could play in my body's ability to recover. I would re-learn this lesson almost exactly four years later.

During my illness, I realized the full extent of Mother's deterioration. Seeing me in the hospital, she seemed to understand my situation. As soon as I returned home, she assumed that everything was back to normal. She and I had been in the habit of "going for a ride" almost every afternoon while Daddy took a nap. Countless times each day I'd have to explain why I didn't feel strong enough for these excursions. I remember thinking, "I can no longer depend on Mother for comfort and support. Her physical presence is still with me, but emotionally *I've lost her.*"

Daddy did not argue with my suggestion that we beef up Mother's support system. We increased Josephine's hours and added two new helpers, Mattie Leach and Liz Murray, both recommended by Josephine. They would be Mother's primary caregivers for the rest of her life.

ONE OF THE THORNIEST PROBLEMS for families facing Alzheimer's is when to confiscate the car keys. In retrospect, I know that Mother continued to drive longer than she should have. She had always been so self-sufficient and independent, we hated to clip her wings prematurely.

The deciding incident occurred one day as she and I approached a red light on a deserted side street in Bennettsville. Mother stopped, looked both ways, and went right through it. She had confused a stoplight with a stop sign. I pointed out her error as gently and tactfully as I could. She bristled, accusing me of trying to tell her how to drive.

When Daddy learned what had happened, he agreed that Mother should not drive anymore. But how could we enforce this? Our strategy was to park the car out of sight and tell her it was in the shop for repairs. She gradually forgot about driving and no longer questioned us about the car.

Mother's final link to tennis was a weekly mixed doubles foursome in Rockingham, North Carolina, a fifty-minute drive from Bennettsville. The other players were about Mother's age and had health problems of their own, which eventually prompted the group to disband. Mother never forgot how to hit the ball and play the game, but she had to rely totally on her partner to keep score.

FAY McLAURIN AND I made a huge hit with our new "Program of American Songs," presented at the Marlboro Civic Center on Sunday afternoon, September 8, 2002. Mary Jo had selected my dress for the occasion, a slinky concoction in vibrant shades of blue and gold. Admonishing me in no uncertain terms to abandon the "little girl style" I usually wore, she said, "Get with it! Show off your figure!"

September 8, 2002: My parents and I are outside the Marlboro Civic Center, Bennettsville, S.C., just after my "Program of American Songs." My publicity picture is visible in the marquee.

Her advice proved fortuitous because a special male friend, Robert Owens, had made the two-hour drive from Raleigh, North Carolina, to be in the audience that day. Robert and I grew up together in Bennettsville. We had attended the same church, the same schools—and we both had spent our entire lives coping with and overcoming congenital physical disabilities. I knew that after Robert's divorce, he had been awarded custody of his adopted son, Terry. Both of them not only attended the performance, but also stayed to speak to me at the reception.

In a few weeks, Robert sent me a letter, asking if he could

come to Bennettsville to take me to lunch. With Josephine cheering me on from the sidelines, I accepted his invitation.

Robert and I immediately felt a strong connection to each other, intellectually and emotionally. It seemed as if our years apart had never happened. We spoke by phone daily, and whenever I came to Bennettsville, we saw each other every weekend. Twice I flew from Cleveland to Raleigh to visit him. Our relationship began to cool when it became apparent that he was interested in marriage, and I wasn't. The "M" word still gave me a severe case of claustrophobia. I think Robert and I will always be good friends. He calls me periodically, and we exchange news with each other.

Unfortunately, Mother did not remember Robert, even though she had known him well during his childhood years and had followed his progress with great interest. In vain, I kept hoping that seeing him on his crutches might trigger some remembrance. Robert understood, of course, but I'm sure he felt a sense of disappointment, as did I.

SEEING THE OPEN SUITCASE ON MOTHER'S BED, I knew she had begun the packing-to-go-home stage of Alzheimer's. At first, I tried to reason with her.

"Mother," I said gently. "You don't have to pack. You're already at home."

"This is home?" she responded incredulously.

"Yes, just look around. See all the pictures of Mary Jo and me? Your favorite spot on the sofa?"

"I guess this *is* home."

"Gee, that was pretty easy," I thought to myself, until a little while later when she was packing again.

Given the futility of rational explanations, we simply let Mother pack whenever she wished. Sometimes several days would pass with no packing at all. We'd think, "Good! That phase is over."

Then, as if obeying some strange signal only she could hear, she'd resume pulling items from drawers and closets and arranging them in careful piles on the bed. We couldn't help smiling over her typical assortment: a variety of mismatched pieces of clothing and usually *one* tennis shoe. Constant access to her purse was an essential part of the ritual. We had long since taken away her credit cards, but we allowed her a small amount of cash. She had to be "ready to go home" at a moment's notice.

Mother often displayed a surprisingly accurate recall of the distant past. Reliving her days as a young girl when she sold tickets at B.B.'s movie theater in Dillon, she'd ask, "Does Daddy want me to work tonight?" I generally answered by saying, "No, Mother, your daddy said you could take tonight off." Two of Mother's childhood friends from Dillon attended my 2002 program at the civic center. She knew them by name and remembered her longstanding relationship with them.

ALTHOUGH I CONTINUED TO DIVIDE MY TIME between my two homes, I gradually lengthened my stays in South Carolina and shortened my stays in Ohio. Josephine, Mattie, and Liz were certainly capable of holding the fort in my absence. However, I felt better when I could observe in person what was happening with Mother, and Daddy's unspoken attitude seemed to be, "As long as Vickie's here, everything will be okay."

Mother's increasingly unpredictable behavior caused some very awkward situations. Mattie told me that one night Mother had questioned her sharply: "Why are you here?" Mattie made the mistake of saying that Daddy wanted her to stay, which caused Mother to leap to the conclusion that Mattie was staying *with Daddy!* "You can't stay with my husband!" she shouted. To escape Mother's wrath, Mattie fled hastily to the living room and hid behind a chair.

In a few minutes, the incident forgotten, Mother went looking for Mattie and seemed completely unfazed at finding her crouched behind a chair. "Are you sure you're comfortable down there?" Mother asked politely.

Holding back laughter, Mattie managed to respond with equal politeness, "Yes, I'm quite comfortable, thank you."

On another occasion, Mary Jo, Jack, and I were visiting Mother and Daddy. Mary Jo unexpectedly entered my bedroom just after I had gone to bed. "What's going on?" I asked.

Between giggles, she explained, "Mother won't let Jack and me share a bedroom because she doesn't think we're married, so I told her I'd sleep with you." Then she added, "But don't worry. Mother will soon be settled for the night, and I can sneak back into the bedroom with Jack." Oh, the trials of having a loved one with Alzheimer's.

EACH TIME I FLEW INTO FLORENCE, SOUTH CAROLINA, I peered through the window of the plane to see my parents inside the terminal, waiting to greet me: Daddy, looking thin and pale; Mother, nestled by his side, holding her purse, smiling in anticipation of my arrival. I could scarcely control the lump in my throat, realizing that despite my best efforts, their lives were inevitably declining. The thought made my own mortality painfully real.

Our concerns for Mother and Daddy notwithstanding, Mary Jo and I agreed that we should not neglect ourselves; we planned a trip to Colorado in late September 2006. I'd fly from Cleveland, Mary Jo from South Carolina, and we'd rendezvous in Denver. The tickets had been purchased, the itinerary was set, but there is an old saying about "the best-laid plans."

When I called Mary Jo on Labor Day to say I felt ill, we had no idea that I faced a life-threatening situation from which she would save me.

THE RIGHT SPIN

My first motorized wheelchair can only be described as a dinosaur. Its most annoying tendency was that it kept moving after my hand released the joystick—a few inches or a few feet—depending on my speed. Catastrophes were inevitable.

Mishaps occurred mostly in the grocery store, where I regularly plunged into displays of Ritz crackers, doughnuts, or canned pineapple. (Those cans hurt when they fall on your feet!) The crash invariably riveted the attention of everyone in sight. Store employees rushed to the scene: "Don't worry! No problem! We can clean this up in a jiffy. This display was blocking the aisle anyway."

But I knew they were thinking, "Please get out of here before you do any more damage!"

Once I got my new, state-of-the-art motorized chair in 2000, there were no more grocery store collisions, because this chair could stop on a dime. So, no more catastrophes, right? Wrong!

One day I entered the mailroom at the apartment building where I lived. The folding door was open, but someone had jarred it, so that it partially blocked the entryway. After retrieving my mail, I glanced behind me. Confident that I had enough clearance, I began to back out into the lobby.

Almost immediately, I heard a *Ccccrrunch* and stopped instantly, but the damage had been done. Completely unhinged, the door lay flat on the floor. I screamed in dismay, noting peripherally that the two other people in the mailroom had vanished.

The office had closed for the day, but early the next morning, tail between my legs, I went to confess my crime. The secretary had no idea what I was apologizing for, so I explained: "The mailroom door—I'm the one who demolished it."

"Is this the door you're referring to?" The building manager had entered the office, holding what was left of the door.

"Yes, that's the one." I quickly added, "I'll be happy to pay for replacing it."

"No, that won't be necessary," he said. He very politely *didn't* say, "But don't let it happen again."

When I told my friend Lue about the incident, I thought she would die laughing.

"Lue!" I said. "This is dreadful! I feel awful."

She replied matter-of-factly: "Vickie, how many years have you lived in this building?"

"Twenty-five."

"And how many times have you destroyed the mail room door?"

"Once."

"Then, I'd say you have an excellent safety record!"

Isn't it great how a friend can put just the right spin on things?

"A PROGRAM OF AMERICAN SONGS" WITH FAY McLAURIN, PIANIST

Marlboro Civic Center
Bennettsville, S.C.
September 8, 2002

Two Spirituals .... arr. Mark Hayes
    Deep River
    Give Me Jesus

The Frozen Logger ....James Stephens

Last Winter's Night .... Alabama Folk Song

Father Grumble .... New England Folk Song

Embraceable You .... Gershwin

Let's Call the Whole Thing Off..................................... Gershwin

Encore: Someone To Watch Over Me .... Gershwin

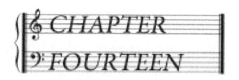

A NEAR DEATH ENCOUNTER,
A NEW SONG

I REMEMBER NOTHING of the onset and early stages of my illness, not even the phone call to Mary Jo, telling her that I wasn't feeling well. The following account has been pieced together entirely from what others have told me.

My initial symptoms were severe nausea and diarrhea. A friend from the apartment building took me to the emergency room of the local hospital, where tests were done. I was sent home with medications to settle my stomach, which, as it turned out, only made the situation worse. The next day, I received a phone call informing me that I had tested positive for an E. coli infection and that I should return to the hospital right away to be admitted for treatment. My aide, Frieda Overton, contacted Mary Jo to tell her what had happened.

Mary Jo knew something was terribly wrong when she called me at the hospital and heard my disjointed, incoherent conversation. I couldn't complete a sentence. She became downright panic-stricken when she spoke to my nurse, who said nonchalantly, "Oh, your sister can talk?" The apparent assumption was that my being in a wheelchair implied mental as well as physical impairment.

Mary Jo exploded: "Of course she can talk! The woman has a doctorate in music! She taught at Baldwin Wallace for over twenty years. She can't walk, but she can damn well finish a sentence! Do something to help her!" There is no doubt in my mind that I owe my very life to her timely intervention.

Within twenty-four hours, an ambulance transported me to University Hospital in Cleveland. By this time, I was comatose. Sepsis had set in, causing my entire body to shut down. The doctors in ICU performed a tracheotomy. I was placed on a respirator. Dialysis restored my kidney function.

Cleansing my system of the infection necessitated a specific IV procedure called *aphaeresis*, which introduces new platelets into the bloodstream. Via telephone, Mary Jo readily gave permission for those treatments to begin.

In the meantime, Mary Jo informed her supervisor at Cryovac (a plastic wrap manufacturer) that she needed to take two weeks of vacation immediately. Anxious and worried, she and Jack made the long drive to Ohio. Whatever the outcome, they would be there to offer me their love and support.

Mary Jo and Jack's first priority was to determine how I had contracted the infection. The State Board of Health had left a message on my answering machine asking that very question. My friends said that in the past few days I had gone to the rec center to walk in the water; I had eaten seafood at a local restaurant; and Frieda had made me a salad for lunch at the apartment. Mary Jo gave the State Board of Health this information, but concluded, "We'll probably never have an answer."

When Mary Jo saw me for the first time in ICU—lying there, unconscious, hooked up to every kind of machine imaginable, my body bloated almost beyond recognition—she burst into tears and ran screaming from the room. My doctors gave her no false hopes. My survival chances were about 50-50. If I did survive, my brain might be permanently damaged. On the positive side, Mary Jo felt reassured not only by the professionalism of the medical team, but also by the fact that University Hospital is a regional center specializing in aphaeresis treatments. I seemed to be in the best possible place to receive the care I needed, but now she was more determined than ever to know what had caused this terrible crisis.

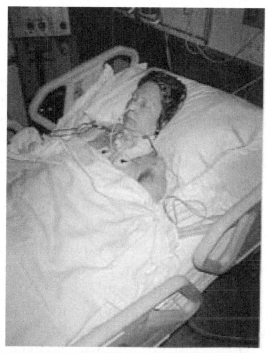

September 2006: My brother-in-law, Jack Harris, took this picture of me while I was unconscious in ICU.

The next night, as Mary Jo and Jack entered the hospital, she glanced at the TV in the lobby. The sound was off; however, an announcement "crawling" across the bottom of the screen riveted her attention. Outbreaks of E. coli had been reported in several locations, including Cleveland, due to tainted spinach. "Jack!" she called out. "This is it. I don't believe in coincidences. We have to find out when and where Vickie has been eating spinach."

Developments came thick and fast. Mary Jo found a partially consumed package of raw spinach in my refrigerator. Frieda confirmed that she had made me a spinach salad for lunch shortly before I got sick. Mary Jo called the State Board of Health. They picked up the spinach in order to test it for E. coli.

Next, Mary Jo and Jack consulted a lawyer. He agreed that if the spinach I had eaten proved to be the "smoking gun," we would have a solid basis for a lawsuit. Urging Mary Jo and Jack to go public with my story, he arranged for them to be interviewed by a local TV news anchor that same day. Mary Jo describes the report, which aired at 11:00 p.m., as being quite dramatic: "Former Baldwin Wallace professor fights for her life at University Hospital." Mary Jo and Jack then issued their stern warning: "Do not, under any circumstances, eat raw spinach!"

Mary Jo had been calling friends and relatives to tell them of my illness. To keep everyone informed of my condition and to save time and energy, she put an updated message on my answering machine each night. From the beginning, many prayers were lifted up on my behalf.

Twice during my comatose month in ICU, Dady Mehta and Marilyn Meeker drove from Ann Arbor to Cleveland to visit me. Martha, who had severe problems with her right knee, came with Dady a few weeks later. The three of them subsequently told me that the sight of my seemingly lifeless form was almost more than they could bear.

A few years earlier, a violinist friend of the Mehtas had awakened from a coma when his favorite recording, Dady's performance of Bach's *Goldberg Variations*, had been played loudly, nonstop, for several days. As Dady stood next to the man's bed, he suddenly opened his eyes, held up one finger, shook it in Dady's face, and said, "Too fast!"

Hoping that the same strategy might work for me, the Mehtas had CDs made of my piano recitals ASAP, and Mary Jo arranged to have a CD player placed in my room. Whenever a new nurse came in, looking puzzled, Mary Jo would explain, "That's one of Vickie's concerts." Although I can offer no concrete proof, my gut-level opinion is that I was subliminally aware of my environment and that the stimulation of being surrounded by music I knew and loved helped bring me back to life.

Mary Jo's two weeks of vacation were drawing to a close, but she did not want to leave until I showed some sign of improvement. That glimmer of hope came one afternoon when Mary Jo and Josie Harris were with me. In strode an extremely handsome young resident to give me an aphaeresis treatment. My gaze never left his face; and, as Mary Jo and Josie watched in amazement, I smiled, inched my body toward the side of the bed where he stood, and began fluttering my eyelashes. Mary Jo turned to Josie and said, "Maybe, just maybe, Vickie is going to be okay."

Mary Jo and Jack drove back to South Carolina so she could resume her job at Cryovac. Shortly thereafter, they learned that the spinach in my refrigerator had tested positive for the identical strain of E. coli that had infected my body. We did indeed have the smoking gun. Jack then returned to Ohio for an additional two weeks. He located my grocery store bonus card, which showed the precise day and time I had bought the spinach. This corroborating information, according to our lawyer, clinched the case.

When Jack left Ohio in early October, my doctors were optimistic that I would soon be out of ICU. Breathing on my own, I was also making an effort to speak despite the aftereffects of the recent tracheotomy. My kidney function, however, had not returned. Frequent dialysis continued.

My thoughts were muddled and confused. Jack still teases me

about the day (of which I have no recollection) when he stood at the foot of my bed, and a nurse asked me to identify him. Without hesitation I said, "Tom Baker!" The only resemblance between the two is a beard. Months later, Josie Harris told me I once called her "Nancy." I must have been reliving my years at the University of Illinois.

Clearly I had come a long way, but I had a long way to go.

ALL OF A SUDDEN, OR SO IT SEEMED, I AWOKE, as if from a nightmare. I struggled to make sense of what people were telling me.

I was in the hospital—because I ate some bad spinach?

How could I be in the hospital and not remember *going* to the hospital?

Had I really been in ICU for nearly a month with my sister, brother-in-law, and good friends by my side? Assuming this to be true, why was my mind a total blank?

I knew my kidneys were not functioning properly because almost every day someone came into my room to take me to dialysis, a dreadfully tedious, tiring process.

I recall the following conversation with a doctor, who leaned over me, examining my abdomen. I asked him, "Why aren't my kidneys working right?"

"Because you've been suffering from a severe infection."

"Will my kidneys ever work right?"

"I hope so, but I can't be sure."

"What if my kidneys never work right? Will I need a transplant?"

"I hope not, but I can't be sure."

I gave up on this decidedly unsatisfactory exchange. My nightmare, I soon discovered, had just begun.

For visitors, I managed some semblance of alertness; otherwise, I languished in a dull stupor. Time meant nothing. Hours, days, and weeks merged into an amorphous haze. I drifted in and out of reality. After vividly imagining myself in my apartment or at my parents' home in Bennettsville, I'd think, "No, I'm not there. I'm in a hospital."

Feeding myself from a tray while lying in a hospital bed had never been my forté. In my weakened state, the challenge proved overwhelming. Furthermore, I had little incentive to eat. Some days my food stayed down. On other days, for no apparent reason, whatever I ate, I threw up. Fortunately, Mary Jo found a Sitters' Service, which, for a modest fee, provided people to assist patients with specific tasks, like eating. This resource was a lifesaver. Gradually, my digestive problems subsided and my kidney function returned, eliminating the need for those onerous dialysis treatments.

Twice my doctors moved me from University Hospital to a nearby rehab facility; twice they vastly overestimated my readiness for the rigors of physical therapy. I'd fall asleep on the exercise mat, and within a few days, I'd be back in the hospital.

When Mary Jo and Jack came to spend Thanksgiving weekend with me, they rejoiced at my progress. After all, when they last saw me, I had been barely conscious in ICU. Jokingly, they complained about the accommodations of my small Ohio apartment. Every night, they drew straws to determine which one would sleep in my single bed; the other would have to take my lumpy sofa. Sharing a laugh with them cheered me, body and soul.

Mary Jo brought with her a beautiful, brightly colored prayer quilt that had been made by a group of women at First United Methodist Church in Bennettsville, who called themselves "The Energetics." Many of these ladies I had known since childhood. I was deeply touched that every stitch represented a prayer for my recovery. Mary Jo wrapped me in the quilt and pushed me, in my bed, to an outdoor courtyard. How I enjoyed the un-characteristically warm November sunshine.

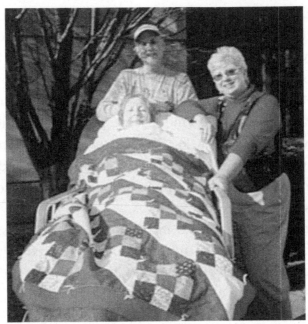

Thanksgiving 2006: in the hospital courtyard with my sister Mary Jo and her husband Jack. They had brought me a prayer quilt made by a group of women from First United Methodist Church in Bennettsville.

That visit marked a turning point for me. I began to consider what to do when I left the hospital. Only for a brief moment did I entertain the obviously ludicrous thought of returning to my apartment. My doctors recommended that I go to a nursing home, where regular physical therapy could restore my strength. Frieda volunteered to investigate facilities near Berea so my friends would be closer to me; she selected a place only a few miles from Tower in the Park. I almost felt as if I were going home. A week before Christmas 2006, I entered the next phase of my recovery with high hopes.

Those hopes soon faded. I cannot describe my four months in the nursing home as a positive experience, although in retrospect, I realize that the facility where I stayed was probably much better than average. It provided a physically attractive, spotlessly clean environment where I received, for the most part, good care. Much of my frustration resulted from unrealistic expectations. I should not have been surprised that the nursing home's rigid schedule (bed baths as early as 5:30 a.m.) took precedence over my urgent need for rest and recuperation.

The physical therapy proved particularly disappointing. Every morning after breakfast, I went to a large room with about fifteen other residents and *one* therapist. We were given simple exercises to perform—but with little direct supervision or individual attention, I made negligible progress and generally felt the time would have been better spent sleeping.

The majority of the nurses' aides were caring and conscientious, with the notable exception of Hilda (not her real name), who actually frightened me. She treated me so roughly, I cringed whenever she entered my room to give me a bed bath. She had told me she played the lottery daily, and I had a purely selfish motive for hoping she'd win: "If you don't show up for work tomorrow, we'll know why."

"Oh, no!" she barked. "I wouldn't quit my job. I love my work."

I could only think, "God help us all if she ever *hates* her work."

THE UNFAILING LOVE AND SUPPORT of friends bolstered my morale. The devotion of the Mehtas seemed truly inexhaustible. Despite Martha's knee pain, they made the two-and-a-half-hour drive from Ann Arbor every two or three weeks. Frieda Overton

229

and Mary Cruz, a relatively new friend at Tower in the Park, took turns assisting me in eating lunch or dinner. Both Mary Gay (widow of my former colleague, Al Gay) and Lue Fletcher's sister, Marie Douglas, brought me yummy homemade egg custard. An elderly friend, who couldn't visit in person, sent me a basket of fresh fruit. I enjoyed periodic visits from Renie, Daniela, Fran (the aide who had been driving me to church before my illness), Josie, Chungsim, Sue and Mel, and others. I also received cards and telephone calls from people in South Carolina. Each one of these wonderful people wanted nothing more than for me to get well, but as the days passed, I concluded that this would never happen as long as I remained in the nursing home. There had been little improvement in my condition—I was merely marking time.

MARY JO AND JACK had built their home in Easley, South Carolina, near Greenville, in 1994. Envisioning a day when I might want to live with them, they included an unfinished basement apartment. Now, some thirteen years later, they offered to finish the project so I could move in ASAP. Initially caught off-guard, I quickly acquiesced. The security of being with my family appealed to me. Moreover, I realized that in light of my serious illness and slow recovery, returning to Tower in the Park would be problematic. Daddy's instant agreement to fund the renovations cinched the deal.

Well in advance of my move, the Mehtas began preparing for the time when I would be able to continue my musical and intellectual growth. They gave me a movable, adjustable book-stand so I could read in bed easily and comfortably. They even went to my apartment at Tower in the Park, gathered all my books, took them to Ann Arbor, had them spiral bound (thus eliminating the need for me to hold them open), and shipped them to Mary Jo's address in Easley. They have since added many volumes to my library, all spiral bound.

BY EARLY MARCH, Mother's condition had deteriorated drastically. I dared to hope she might still be alive on April 21, the target date for my move. Those hopes were dashed when Mary Jo called on March 19 to say that she thought Mother was ready to die but wanted to hear from me before "letting go." Mary Jo warned me that Mother would probably not be able to speak and might not recognize my voice. Still, I had to make the effort. I had to pull myself together and just do it.

Josephine's sister, Jackie, a hospice nurse, answered the phone. When she held the receiver to Mother's ear, I heard the sound of heavy, labored breathing, but as soon as I identified myself, there was silence. Once I started talking, I had to keep talking; otherwise, I would have fallen apart, which wouldn't have done Mother or me any good. I told Mother I loved her and that she had always been the best Mother I could have ever wanted or wished for. I concluded by saying, "You've lived a long, full life. If you're tired and ready to rest, it's okay to leave this world."

Jackie assured me that Mother had known exactly who I was and had listened intently to every word I said. Mother died the next day.

My feelings were a mixture of sadness, frustration, and anger. Mother's life and mine had been so closely intertwined, I almost felt as if a part of me had died with her. She had nurtured, supported, and loved me unconditionally. She had been my companion, caregiver, confidante, and friend. It now seemed incredible that circumstances totally beyond my control would deny me the closure of attending her funeral. She had died, and I couldn't be there to say goodbye. I could do nothing but grieve— grieve over the loss of my mother, grieve over the futility and unfairness of the situation.

SHORTLY BEFORE I LEFT FOR SOUTH CAROLINA, my lawyers brought a man to the nursing home to make a video documenting my condition. I spoke candidly about my illness and the difficulties I still faced. Viewing the finished product sent me into shock. I looked horribly old; my usually strong, confident voice sounded weak and tentative. For the first time, I grasped the seriousness of my predicament: I was an invalid.

My lawyers had hired a woman with the enigmatic title of Life Planner. At first, we had no idea what she would do, but her expertise proved indispensable. When I arrived in Easley, I had already been accepted as a patient by an excellent doctor at Internal Medicine Associates of Greenville, and a home health agency in Easley had agreed to provide round-the-clock aides for my care.

All other aspects of the move fell on Mary Jo's shoulders—a task of Herculean proportions. She told me later that just when she'd be on the verge of a nervous breakdown, from somewhere, she'd find the strength to carry on, as if the hand of Divine Providence were leading her. She located an organization in Cleveland that supplies travel companions to people who are sick or disabled. (I qualified on both counts.) For a fee of $100, a woman flew with me from Cleveland to Atlanta. When Mary Jo and Jack met us at the airport, I think they were taken aback by my limp, lethargic state. Totally exhausted from the trip, I spoke hardly a word during the drive back to Easley. I was simply grateful to be going to my new home.

I IMMEDIATELY APPRECIATED the coziness and comfort of my apartment. Beautiful, vibrant colors greeted me. Mary Jo and Jack had selected a sunny yellow for the hallway, kitchen, and bathroom; powdery blue for the bedroom; and for the living room, a deep, rich red, which, Mary Jo pointed out, offered the perfect dramatic contrast to my shiny black grand piano. I agreed. My belongings, piano included, appeared to have made the move from Ohio in good shape. I noticed my books on the bedroom shelves. Mary Jo showed me the catalogue prepared by the Mehtas, listing each title in the same order as its shelf arrangement. Absolutely everything, it seemed, had been made ready for me.

What a wonderful luxury to have my very own support system! No more adapting to the constraints of a hospital or nursing home schedule, and someone was always available to help me eat whatever I wanted, as much as I wanted. Amen to that.

Two of my aides, Darlene Clark (first shift) and Ellen Richards (third shift), began their duties on Day One. Various people filled the second shift slot until mid-May, when Pam Rivard came on board, rounding out my weekday schedule. These three marvelous women became loyal friends and have been the mainstays of my support system for over three years.

As for the weekend aides supplied by the agency—suffice it to say that they were not cut from the same cloth as Darlene, Pam, and Ellen. When Mary Jo's complaints produced no tangible improvement, we knew something had to be done, but what?

In the meantime, Mary Jo faced a dilemma at Cryovac: begin working third shift on a regular basis or lose her job. Commiserating, we arrived at a win-win solution for both of us. If Mary Jo retired from Cryovac, she could serve as my weekend aide. I'd pay her the money we were currently wasting on the useless people from the agency. Since she preferred not to be "on call" through the night, we found a local woman to stay with me every Saturday evening; she in turn introduced us to her two nieces, who worked alternate Sunday evenings. Mary Jo and I heartily congratulated ourselves on our ingenuity and good old-fashioned common sense.

During my first six weeks in South Carolina, I did little but sleep—peaceful, blissful, heavenly sleep. Almost every afternoon, Mary Jo pushed me in my wheelchair to the backyard flower garden, where I'd promptly fall asleep. Going to doctors' appointments with Darlene, I'd doze off before the car had left the driveway. Darlene quieted Mary Jo's alarm by explaining that sleep was my body's natural and necessary way of healing itself.

The home health agency sent a registered nurse to give me weekly checkups and dispense my prescription medications. A physical therapist came twice a week and showed Darlene how to perform range-of-motion exercises on my limbs as I lay on the bed.

"Fragile" best describes my emotional as well as my physical condition. Perhaps unconsciously, I had believed that moving to Easley would magically restore me to good health. When this didn't happen, I allowed doubt and uncertainty to take over. What did the future hold? Had I made the right decision in uprooting myself from a familiar environment in which I had flourished for many years? Would I ever flourish again? How could I build a new life for myself when I could hardly get out of bed?

My unresolved feelings of grief over Mother's death complicated the picture. Listening to a tape of the funeral service and looking at funeral photographs taken by a friend provided some closure. It helped tremendously when Mary Jo confided in me that Mother had appeared to her in a dream, had smiled, and embraced her. I told Mary Jo that no doubt Mother was extremely proud of her not only for saving my life, but also for inviting me to share her home. I added that I was proud of her too—and grateful beyond words. We hugged each other and wept.

For me, physical healing and emotional adjustment were interrelated, step-by-step processes. I wanted to regain control of my life, but first I had to believe that recovery was possible. Eight months earlier, I had been largely independent, requiring only minimal assistance with certain tasks. Now I lay flat on my back, unable even to turn on my side in the bed without help. I awoke each morning with the bleak realization that my "new" life in Easley, although infinitely preferable to the nursing home environment, left much to be desired.

Proper rest, nourishing food, and the right medications gradually enabled me to think more clearly about my situation. Lying in bed gave me ample time for prayer and soul-searching. I contemplated the fundamental values that had been instilled in me from my earliest years. First and foremost, I had always believed—and still believed—in a benevolent God and in the intrinsic goodness of life. During the darkest days of my illness, Mary Jo had felt the presence of a Divine Hand, leading her to make the decisions that had resulted in my survival. The words of Psalm 23 drifted into my mind: "Though I walk through the valley of the shadow of death, I will fear no evil, for thou art with me. Surely goodness and mercy will follow me all the days of my life." By the grace of God, my life had been spared. The next step was up to me. My quality of life would be restored if and when I chose to rehabilitate myself.

I thought of Mother: her competitive spirit on the tennis court, her zest for fun and adventure, her incredible will to live in the face of advancing Alzheimer's. Would she not want me to fight for my quality of life? No, she would *expect* me to fight for my quality of life!

At last, I realized that my doctors were right when they emphasized that time would ultimately be on my side. Throughout my life, obstacles had never been overcome quickly or easily, but they had been overcome. Why should my present circumstances be any different? Putting aside unrealistic expectations, I would have to rely on the virtues that had served me well in the past—faith, hope, and especially patience. The time had come to embrace the future. With God's help and the support of the people around me, I would learn a new song.

DADDY'S WEEKEND VISIT with us in Easley had ended with this advice: "Vickie, you have to move your body as much as you possibly can." I promised to do my best. In recent years, walking in chest-deep water had been an enjoyable and beneficial form of exercise for me, so this seemed a logical way to start.

Darlene took me to the indoor pool at the local YMCA, where Mary Jo and Jack are members. Like the pool I had used in Berea, this one is equipped with a chair lift to lower me into and raise me out of the water. At first, Darlene had to get into the pool and support me while I made a valiant (and not terribly successful) effort to balance myself and maneuver my legs. After several weeks, we began to see progress, and the very act of doing something made me feel better. If "the journey of a thousand miles begins with a single step," I had just taken that all-important first step.

As my coordination improved, I walked in the water by myself with Darlene keeping a watchful eye from the side of the pool. One day, a woman who swam there regularly approached Darlene to ask about me. Having noticed my solemn, silent demeanor, she asked the nature of my disability and wondered whether I could talk. Darlene, who never sees a stranger, launched into my whole life story: "Vickie used to be a concert pianist ... She taught piano for many years at a college in Ohio ... She's now recuperating from a nearly-fatal illness, etc."

The woman ventured shyly, "I'm a piano teacher. Do you think Vickie would mind if I asked her some questions?"

"I think she'd love it!" Darlene exclaimed.

My friendship with Deb Edson would play a decisive role in my recovery. Recalling our first conversation in the pool, she says that when she mentioned the word *music*, I smiled—the first time she had ever seen me smile—and my face lit up like a Christmas tree. I had found a fellow musician with whom I could "talk shop." A crucial piece of my identity had been restored.

In late spring 2007, a settlement was reached with the companies responsible for the tainted spinach. Mary Jo had wisely decided not to seek a specific dollar amount: "All we want is for Vickie to have the support system she needs for the rest of her life." Since the settlement money covers those expenses, we are satisfied, although nothing can fully compensate for the trauma we suffered.

I WAS THRILLED when Nancy Stagg called to tell me she'd be driving through South Carolina at the end of June. My limited stamina detracted not one iota from the joy of her visit. She simply pulled a chair next to my bed, allowing me to rest and chat simultaneously. She wanted to hear the details of my illness, but we quickly moved on to a myriad of topics ranging from cosmology to religion to reminiscences of the "old days" at the University of Illinois. Jack prepared a delicious dinner for us. I had to laugh as Nancy, a would-be vegetarian, devoured a thick, juicy steak.

About a week prior to Nancy's visit, Darlene had seen a former patient of hers at the YMCA pool; two physical therapists were assisting the man. Since she and I had previously discussed the possibility of my getting "official" therapy (to supplement my walking in the water), she approached the team and learned that they worked for Dosher Physical Therapy Associates in Easley. Yes, they were accepting new patients. I called and set up a consultation for July 5.

Mike Dosher obviously knew his stuff. Listening intently to the saga of my physical problems—congenital disability, rheumatoid arthritis, E. coli infection—he took notes and asked perceptive, intelligent questions. I gave him detailed information about my capabilities and limitations at each stage of my life. He readily assessed for himself the severity of my current limitations. When he inquired about my goals for the future, I said, "I want to be able to turn on my side in bed without assistance." He wisely made no promises, but expressed confidence that I could achieve this and more. "Okay!" I said, with more optimism than I'd felt in a long time. "When do we start?" His answer: "As soon as you get a prescription from your doctor, so your insurance companies can be billed for the cost." I liked this young man already.

Prescription in hand, I showed up for my first appointment with a mixture of anticipation and anxiety. No stranger to challenges, I had a feeling this just might be one of the biggest I'd ever faced.

That premonition was right on the money. Physical therapy, properly done, is methodical, systematic, and tough. As in learning to play a musical instrument, there are no shortcuts. In order to rebuild my trunk muscles, I executed hundreds, if not thousands, of bridges and crunches. I extended and lifted my legs with weights strapped to my ankles. I stood at the parallel bars. I flexed my arms against the resistance of elastic bands. Then came my first attempt at balancing myself while sitting on a ball. I squealed in terror, as Mike laughingly accused me of "speaking in tongues."

Mike nearly had a heart attack the day his partner, Keith Carter, took it upon himself to put me on the leg press machine. (Mike's reservations stemmed from the fact that my right hip is socketless.) Since I suffered no ill effects, Mike added the leg press to my routine, with a word of caution: "Don't overdo it."

Monumental Milestone No. 1 occurred in mid-September. One night I did, in fact, turn on my side in bed by myself. Such was my euphoria that I didn't get another wink of sleep that night. I just lay there *on my side*, smiling. When I told Mike, he hugged me: "Oh, Vickie! This is so major!"

Monumental Milestone No. 2 came a few months later when I got out of bed by myself and transferred to my wheelchair. At first, I had asked my aides not to share this accomplishment with Mary Jo because I wanted to wait until I felt more confident. Then, one morning, Darlene came into my bedroom and whispered, "It's show time." Mary Jo and the nurse from the home health agency were in the kitchen, so Darlene invited them to "come and see something amazing." Slowly, cautiously, I raised myself up off the bed, pivoted, and plopped into my chair—not the most graceful of maneuvers, but I did it. Applause and cheers filled the room. I had just given one of my finest performances, if I do say so myself.

MARY JO AND I joined the congregation of Easley Presbyterian Church in September 2007. Almost immediately, Dr. Ralph Boggess, the organist and music director, called me to ask in what ways I might participate in the church's music program. Apparently, Mary Jo had submitted a form telling of my background. I explained that I could no longer play the piano, but that both Mary Jo and I would be interested in singing with the choir. I also told him I preferred to delay making that commitment until my health had improved.

A different but equally promising opportunity literally landed in my lap when my new friend from the pool, Deb Edson, asked me to be her mentor. Not knowing exactly what she had in mind, I agreed without hesitation.

We decided to meet at my apartment on Friday afternoons with a totally open agenda, that is, any music-related or teaching-related topic. During the past three years, we've discussed everything from chord structures to pedaling to stylistic interpretation. Our sessions became even more stimulating and rewarding as she began asking me to listen not only to teaching pieces, but also repertoire that she herself wanted to learn.

Deb's thirteen students played their 2007 Christmas recital in my living room—a lively, hectic, thoroughly delightful occasion. How could I not be inspired by these eager, enthusiastic, talented young pianists? For the post-performance party, each student contributed a plate of homemade goodies, and I got to keep the leftovers. My illness had in no way diminished my sweet tooth.

WEEKLY CHOIR REHEARSALS were added to Mary Jo's and my schedule in the winter of 2008. Although she had not been required to read music for many years, she has relished the demands of learning difficult alto parts. Being a soprano, I have an easier time—just follow the top line! To my great disappointment, however, I discovered that my singing voice is weaker in volume and lower in range than before the E. coli illness. I suspect that the tracheotomy adversely affected my vocal cords. Perhaps a voice therapist could restore the lost resonance and give me back my high notes; but for the present, I am content to add my small voice to a chorus of others, who invariably make me sound good. Singing the Vivaldi *Gloria* with string quartet, organ, and timpani is a thrill I won't soon forget.

After church, Mary Jo and I made a habit of having lunch at one of our favorite local restaurants. On several occasions, people I didn't recognize came to our table, introduced themselves, and said that they too had been going to Dosher's for physical therapy. They wanted to congratulate me on my extraordinary progress. One woman said my positive attitude had given her the incentive she needed to stick to her own regimen. Another woman told me how much she had enjoyed the spectacle of my not-so-delicate balancing act on that ridiculous ball. These observations took me by surprise; I had been totally unaware that I was being watched.

ONE MORNING IN MAY—thirteen months after my move to Easley—I woke up, looked at my bedroom windows, and thought, "I'm not crazy about those curtains. I'd prefer a different color. And why is that picture hanging on this wall? It should be on the opposite wall. I'll ask Darlene to take me shopping—I could use some new clothes for spring."

When I began acting on these thoughts, Darlene, quite concerned, went to Mary Jo: "Vickie's behavior has changed drastically. I think she may be having a nervous breakdown. She's talking a mile a minute, and she's spending money like crazy, buying new things for the apartment, buying new clothes ... "

Before Darlene could finish the sentence, Mary Jo burst out laughing: "This is wonderful! Vickie's back—she's really back! This is the Vickie I've known and loved."

THE TASK OF SORTING THROUGH AND REORGANIZING the contents of my desk revealed a treasure trove of mail that had been sent to me during the early stages of my illness.

The envelopes had been opened, but I did not remember having seen any of it before. Family, friends, BW colleagues, former students—all had expressed their concern for me and their fervent hope that I would make a full recovery. Several mentioned my "fighting spirit," which I would need now more than ever. A friend from Tower in the Park wrote, "Vickie, I know you can't pray for yourself. But don't worry, we'll do the praying for you."

Some of the cards were humorous. My favorite showed a hunky dude on the front: "This is Dan. He's here to administer your medications." On the inside was a scrawny, bald man: "And this is Joe. He's here to give you a bed bath!"

Particularly poignant was a note from Daddy, whose handwritten letters are truly collectors' items: "Your mother and I are deeply saddened by your misfortune. We wish that we were closer so that we could help. Know that we love you and look forward to your recovery." The second page contained a sweet message from Josephine: "You are my hero and I love you. Be strong and keep the faith and believe that God is with you. I can't wait until you get home so I can spoil you."

I felt I had to respond to this tremendous outpouring of support and encouragement. Since my left hand, my "writing" hand, was still relatively weak, I dictated my messages to my aide, Pam, but I signed my own name to each one. I also called Helen Rathburn in the Baldwin Wallace Office of College Relations and asked her to send an email to the BW community, summarizing my progress and thanking everyone for their concern and their prayers.

DEAN SANDERS'S STOPOVER in Easley on June 25, 2008, coincided perfectly with my newfound *joie de vivre*. I couldn't have been happier to celebrate my recovery with a dear friend and former teacher. Dean loved my apartment and took great delight in meeting Mary Jo, Jack, Darlene, and Pam. He brought me a little church mouse sculpture by Kentucky artist Richard Kolb, whose designs are crafted from scrap metal. This charming creature, promptly dubbed "Dean," sits on my kitchen windowsill.

Mike Dosher released me from supervised physical therapy in August 2008, but he urged me to continue my exercise regimen via a gym membership whereby, for a monthly fee, I could come during office hours to use his equipment. He and his associates would be available for consultation if needed. This sounded like a good deal to me. I could ill afford to lose the strength and endurance I had worked so arduously to build up over the past thirteen months.

Despite my phenomenal progress, I realized that I would probably never regain the level of independence I had enjoyed before the E. coli illness. From now on, I would require assistance with many daily chores and activities. Nevertheless, my gradual, steady recovery had brought me back from near death to an active, productive, somewhat normal life. My prayers and the prayers of my family and friends had indeed been answered.

Having re-established my overall physical health, I turned my attention to my eyes and teeth, which had been sorely neglected during my time in the hospital and nursing home. Cataract surgery on both eyes restored a clear palette of vivid color to my vision.

The teeth presented a trickier situation. I had lost a bridge that served as the only reliable chewing spot in the lower part of my mouth. My dentist in Greenville recommended that I get two implants on each side, which would ensure comfortable chewing for the rest of my life. The whole tedious process took about eighteen months, but the absolutely perfect results exceeded my expectations. Whenever I go to my dentist for checkups, he says, "I still can't believe we pulled it off, but we did."

THE HOME HEALTH AGENCY informed Mary Jo that on September 1, 2008, its hourly rates would go up substantially. We were horrified to learn that my aides would receive none of this increase. Mary Jo pored over the contract, including the fine print, and discovered that for "x" number of dollars, we could "buy" employees from the agency and hire them privately. That is exactly what we did, because Mary Jo's calculations showed that we could offer Darlene, Pam, and Ellen a hefty raise and still, in the long run, save money over what we were paying the agency. The private arrangement has proved ideal for everyone.

IN DECEMBER, FOR THE FIRST TIME SINCE MY ILLNESS, I wrote personal notes in my own hand to the seventy-plus people on my Christmas card list, thereby unleashing a flood of congratulatory messages from my friends. The sight of my familiar, if still somewhat shaky, handwriting represented a visible, tangible symbol of my recovery. My aide Pam, on the other hand, said she actually missed taking my correspondence from dictation. She had gotten quite a kick out of acquainting herself with my fascinating assortment of pen pals.

That Christmas season also marked Mary Jo's and my first appearance on the Greenville cultural scene. We attended the annual holiday concert by the Greenville Symphony Orchestra at the Peace Center for the Performing Arts. We've since enjoyed an all-Mozart program by the orchestra and a recital by renowned soprano, Renée Fleming.

THE RESOLUTION OF MY E. COLI CRISIS prompted my momentous decision in April 2009 to resume work on my memoir, which I had started eight years earlier, when I took a class in "Writing Your Personal History" through BW's Institute for Learning in Retirement. With fear and trembling, I dusted off my laptop, knowing that my marginal computer skills were in no way adequate for the task ahead.

I could use my left hand to write the rough draft, but would depend on my voice-activation software, Dragon Naturally-Speaking Professional, for dictating the text into the computer. It was imperative that I open Microsoft Word and Dragon Naturally-Speaking simultaneously, but I'd never understood how to accomplish this. When a friend in Ohio (supposedly a computer expert) couldn't figure it out either, I gave up in despair. Darlene's offer to help seemed like "too little, too late," but within an hour, she had unraveled and explained the whole process. With her as my invaluable computer consultant, I have managed to complete what is probably the last big project of my life.

MY FORMER STUDENT JOHN MRAMOR had told me about his new composition, a suite for piano called *Days*. As a Christmas present in 2009, he sent me a copy of the score. I read the following words on the title page: "To my dear friend, Victoria, to whom I owe a debt of gratitude for inspiring me, supporting me, and for always believing in me. You are loved!" Only one regret marred that proud, happy, satisfying moment—my inability to go to the piano and play the composition that had been dedicated to me.

DADDY STAYED STRONG as long as Mother needed him, but his health began to decline rapidly after her death. Growing thinner and weaker, he suffered several nasty falls. A lifetime of pipe smoking had led to lung problems, necessitating the use of oxygen to ease his breathing at night. When Mary Jo, Jack, and I suggested that he move to Easley, he insisted on remaining in his own home. We acquiesced, with the understanding that he maintain a 24/7 support system for his safety and our peace of mind. He reluctantly agreed.

Every two or three weeks, someone from the family drove to Bennettsville to check on Daddy. If all of us descended on him at once, he felt overwhelmed, so we took turns. Sometimes Mary Jo and Jack went together, sometimes separately, or one of my aides took me. In the course of these excursions, both Darlene and Pam became quite fond of Daddy, and he genuinely appreciated their thoughtfulness and concern.

Daddy retained his mental acuity, taking great pleasure in my recovery and in the fact that his daughters were now together in the same household. He read the first few chapters of my memoir, correcting some of the details in the early chapters and providing an accurate description of the device he and his buddies had devised for getting my wheelchair into my car.

For his nintieth birthday on February 3, 2009, Mary Jo and I invited a few friends and neighbors to his home. They showered him with cards and gag gifts. Josephine made one of her famous pound cakes, and I brought a sweet potato cake from a Greenville restaurant. Daddy had so much fun that he said, "I think I'll have another birthday in about six months. Why wait a whole year?"

By the next February, Daddy's condition had deteriorated sharply. Even with continuous use of oxygen, he sometimes struggled to breathe. Mary Jo and I made a game effort to celebrate with him, but I think he knew that it would be his last birthday. Before leaving to return to Easley, I went into the den, where he had been dozing in his recliner. He spoke very softly but clearly: "I'm proud of you girls." I struggled to hold back the tears.

In mid-May, Darlene and I arrived at Daddy's house to find him gasping for air. Josephine, obviously worried, told us the breathing treatments seemed not to be working. Overriding Daddy's objections, we had him taken by ambulance to a hospital in Florence, where his doctor offered this candid assessment: "If I could instantly make your father thirty years younger and give him a new heart and new lungs, I'd say he might recover. But I can't do any of those things. The most we can do is try to keep him comfortable for whatever time he has left."

Daddy's three-day hospitalization did bring him some relief. By the time he went home, I had made arrangements for a hospital bed to be set up in his den and for him to receive hospice care.

EARLY IN THE MORNING on Thursday, July 1, 2010, Josephine called Mary Jo and Jack. She said that for two days Daddy had refused food and medications. He had not spoken, but repeatedly pointed to Mary Jo's and my picture on the wall. Mary Jo relayed this news to me, and within an hour, we were in the car on our way to Bennettsville. Jack would follow shortly in his truck.

A tired, distraught Josephine met us at the door and led us into the den. We had visited Daddy on Father's Day just a few weeks before, but now he looked terrifyingly frail and emaciated. We knew the end was near. Mary Jo and I stood on either side of his bed, each of us holding one of his hands. I noticed his remarkably firm grip. Making no attempt to talk, he gazed at us intently. We told him we loved him and that he should not worry about us, that we were going to be okay because we had each other and would always take care of each other. Jack arrived and spent a few minutes with him. Daddy closed his eyes as if to rest, so we made our way to the kitchen. In a little while, Josephine went to see if he needed anything. He was gone.

By the time Mary Jo and I left Bennettsville at 5:30 p.m. that day, we had scheduled the visitation for Friday evening at a local funeral home and the funeral service and burial for Saturday afternoon. We were not able to have a military presence at the burial, but the flag-draped coffin paid fitting tribute to his service in the U.S. Navy during World War II.

Complying with our request that Daddy's eulogy contain some elements of humor, the minister told the following true story, which I had never heard: One day Daddy showed up at Bennettsville's leading car dealership to buy a new truck. After selecting the model he wanted, he asked the salesman if the horn from his old truck could be transferred to the new truck. "Of course," the young man answered, but he was curious as to why Daddy had made this seemingly odd request.

Daddy responded in his leisurely Southern style: "Well, you see, it's like this—I've got a herd of beef cattle. Every day, I drive my truck into the pasture to see how they're doing. They recognize my horn and come running. Can you imagine their confusion if they hear a strange-sounding horn?" Everyone at the funeral burst out laughing.

The minister concluded the service by reading a poem Mary Jo had composed and presented to Daddy for Father's Day the previous year:

> My dad's a farmer
> And a real charmer.
> He lights his pipe to smoke
> While telling a joke.
> Daily his garden he tends
> So produce he can give his friends.
> The weather report he gets every day
> Though he no longer has to bale hay.
> He now uses a bucket to get on his tractor –
> His being 90 might be a small factor.
> Strictly old school,
> He lives by the Golden Rule.
> He lives a simple life, helping his neighbor,
> Leading by example, never shirking hard labor.
> To have him as my dad, I'm thankful as can be.
> I only hope he can be as proud of me.

The process of emptying Daddy's house could hardly have gone more smoothly. Mary Jo and I quickly determined the items we wanted to keep. She and I each took one of the china cabinets from the dining room, so at last, all of my miniature pianos are safely housed and beautifully displayed together. My favorite piece of furniture had been the antique bed (from the mid-1800s) that Mother had placed in the guest bedroom. It now graces my guest bedroom. After Mary Jo made her selections, we donated much of the remaining furniture to friends and neighbors.

Daddy's health had been declining for well over a year, yet his death caught me off-guard. I suppose one is never prepared to be an orphan. Nevertheless, I am grateful that both of my parents had long, full lives. Their memory comforts and sustains me daily.

DARLENE AND I FLEW TO MICHIGAN on Friday, August 27, for a weekend with the Mehtas. They had, of course, been following my recovery step-by-step. I had sent them pictures; we had telephoned each other frequently; but they said only a face-to-face meeting would assure them I really was okay. I was equally anxious to see them. My time with Martha and Dady is always stimulating and enjoyable, and I knew that celebrating my recovery with them would be superlative in every way.

Since Mary Jo could not make the trip, I asked Darlene to accompany me. Her initial reluctance (she had never flown before.) soon gave way to her innate spirit of adventure. I prayed as hard as I could for on-time, uneventful, turbulence-free flights, and that's exactly what we had. Darlene gushed, "This is the best way to travel!"

Marilyn Meeker met us at the airport and took us to our hotel. Martha and Dady's house is not wheelchair accessible, although I discovered later that I could enter the lovely, spacious piano studio by way of a side door ramp that had been rented specifically for my use.

After we had unpacked and gotten settled, Dady joined us for lunch in the hotel dining room. "I can't believe you're actually here! You look better than ever!" Dady exclaimed. Darlene asked about the years when Dady and I had been teacher-and-student at St. Andrews College. He told her how he had actually dreaded meeting me back in 1966 because he had heard about my disability and couldn't imagine how I could successfully establish a career in piano. "Of course," he said, "as soon as Vickie began to play, my doubts totally disappeared. By the way, did you know that a whole year passed before she played a wrong note?" I sat

August 27, 2010: with Dady and Martha Mehta at their home in Ann Arbor, Michigan.

there smiling, listening to these familiar narratives, thinking how blessed and fortunate I had been to have friends like the Mehtas—as well as many others who had loved and supported me at every stage of my life. It was an immensely gratifying moment.

Later that afternoon, Martha greeted me with a big hug: "Vickie, Vickie, Vickie!" (She sometimes speaks in triple meter.) "It's so good to see you!" When I voiced my concern that my visit might be too taxing for her, given her knee problems, she corrected me emphatically: "Absolutely not. Your visit is exactly what I need to cheer me up." Both she and Dady instantly took Darlene to their hearts, expressing gratitude for all that she does for me and pronouncing her officially my guardian angel. Marilyn went with us for dinner to a local restaurant specializing in Thai cuisine. Darlene and I had no idea what to order, but we were delighted with the dishes recommended by the Mehtas and devoured every morsel on our plates.

The next day, Marilyn drove all of us from Ann Arbor to Grand

Rapids, where some of Dale Chihuly's gorgeous glass sculptures were on display at the Meijer Sculpture Gardens and Park. Darlene and I were not acquainted with Chihuly's work, but we immediately became ardent admirers. Even Martha's bad knee did not prevent her from hiking around the park with us, as we were awed and inspired by the amazing, mesmerizing displays of colors and shapes. A truly jaw-dropping moment occurred when we got our first glimpse of one of the park's permanent statues, the largest bronze horse in the United States. Darlene took a picture of me beneath its gigantic raised hoof; I look like an ant about to be squashed. A scrumptious Italian meal brought our outing to a relaxed conclusion.

On Sunday afternoon, the Mehtas invited a small group of close friends to the studio for an hour or so of refreshments and conversation. Three hours later, we were still laughing and talking. These were people I had heard of through the years; they in turn said they'd heard of me. Now, at long last, we had the satisfaction of meeting each other in person. My announcement to the group that I had resumed work on my memoir prompted cheers and applause. "But," I hastened to add, "can I count on all of you to buy copies when it's published?" A chorus of positive affirmations filled the room.

Among the guests was Heiju Packard, a superb artist who designs and weaves her own tapestries. Before the party, Martha and Dady showed me photographs of her beautiful creations and asked me to choose the one that would look best in my apartment; it would be their gift to me. When I greeted Heiju, I had the pleasure of telling her that "Break of Day" would soon be my very own prized possession.

The Mehtas suggested that we go to a Mediterranean restaurant for dinner; it would be our third consecutive night of elegant wining and dining. Darlene and I agreed that we could not have been welcomed more warmly. From start to finish, the weekend had been filled with moments of pure, unmitigated joy.

I use the word *joy* deliberately. Unlike the often frivolous, sometimes trivial "happiness" of youth, *joy* carries a deeper, more profound connotation. *Joy* speaks to maturity and experience— the experience of having transcended doubt, disappointment, illness, and adversity. It speaks to serenity—the serenity of knowing that life's vicissitudes cannot destroy one's inner core, one's soul.

"Yes," I thought to myself, "from where I sit, life is not only good—overwhelmingly, undeniably good—it is also overwhelmingly, undeniably *joyful.*"

ABOUT THE AUTHOR

Victoria Covington was born and raised in Bennettsville, South Carolina. She has spent much of her life facing and overcoming physical challenges, adversity, and illness.

She holds music degrees from St. Andrews University in Laurinburg, North Carolina, and the University of Illinois at Urbana-Champaign. In addition to a one-year faculty appointment at UIUC, she was a professor of piano at Baldwin Wallace University in Berea, Ohio, from 1976-99. All proceeds from the sale of her memoir will benefit scholarship programs at these schools.

Vickie now resides at The Woodlands, a retirement community near Furman University in Greenville, South Carolina. She studies voice, audits history and religion courses at Furman, and participates in OLLI (Osher Lifelong Learning Institute) classes.

Her hobbies include reading, attending concerts, and going out to lunch with friends.

Interested readers are encouraged to contact her by e-mail: rollingturtle@att.net.

CPSIA information can be obtained
at www.ICGtesting.com
Printed in the USA
LVOW04s2153171215
467075LV00019B/1454/P